A

Diary Of

Questionable

Journeys

By Vicki Honeycutt

ISBN 978-0-6151-6102-0

This book is dedicated to the loving memory of my dear friend John E. Kelly III. Even though we met only months prior to his passing on this go around, it was very clear to me that John and I have lived many lives together. Instead of grieving his death I choose to honor the healing lessons he taught me and the time we shared. He helped me understand what it means to be a cop, and how one's judgment sometimes gets clouded by their passion for what they believe is justice. John has always been, and will always be in my heart.

Forward

If there is one thing I need for everyone to know before reading this book, it's that none of these people portrayed are likely the same as they were when these events occurred. We have all grown and changed, and would not necessarily react in the same ways now. No one was bad; they just played their role in the manner that the universe intended. I place no blame, feel no guilt, and cherish each second that has brought me to where I am today. None of the things I say or describe are meant as indictments or judgments; it is just my version of reality as I perceived it at the time. I humbly thank everyone for the lessons imparted, and wish them nothing but love and light.

Namaste!

Chapter 1

How did I get here?

It was nothing short of ironic that this girl who refused to shower in an open locker room was dancing practically naked in front of a packed house. Race week in Daytona Beach brings untold numbers of horny men to Pure Gold, the club where she worked as an unlikely stripper. Six months ago she was a plain, but slightly deviant college student who never in her wildest dreams imagined that her glittery, disrobed body would eventually command center stage. The events that brought her here would soon pale in comparison to those which were about to unfold.

I'm not sure if I'm sad or excited to tell you that this is my story. My name is Vicki.

The preceding 18 years of my life were unremarkable at best. For the most part, I watched them from the sidelines. I was quiet and dark, always certain that I was destined for something and somewhere far more interesting than the backward New England town where I grew up.

It will become needless to say that I never quite fit in with the other children, although they did seem to look at me with an oddly petrified reverence. I was admired, but not embraced.

My handful of friends were colorful, artsy, and similarly displaced for one reason or another. We lived in a tiny, mildly affluent Massachusetts town with a big ego problem. People there seemed to be cursed with huge heads, but small minds.

Maybe it was the result of the lack of contemporary relationships that caused me to be curiously close to my grandparents. They were hearty people, having survived the depression. Their generation embodied everything that I longed for: "happily" married couples with strong ties to their extended families and ethnic heritage, hard working dads and stay at home moms, Sunday dinners, big holidays, and, most importantly, a sense of contentment even though they had very little wealth. It's no wonder that they shaped me in the way that they did. I always felt like I was a kindred spirit to them, but born at the wrong time.

My maternal grandmother, Grandma Christie, was my idol. She was a chain-smoking cocktail waitress from Brooklyn, with huge, perky tits, even as she grew old. It always puzzled me why she stayed in her marriage, but I guess it afforded her stability, and the opportunity to see the world while he waited at home. She was the life of the party with her fascinating accounts of her globetrotting adventures. I wanted to be her, with the teased up hair, overdone makeup, big boobs, and unabashed Italian love for everything opulent. She was so alive! Men bowed to her. Well, that is, if you don't include my grandfather, who didn't appreciate her until she was in the ground.

Grandpa Christie influenced me, too. He told me I was fat and ugly, and had a creepy habit of peeking through the bathroom window when I was showering. He was crass and mean, but quick witted and very funny. Luckily, he mellowed with age, and I was able to connect with him as a teenager. As abusive as he could be, he was the only strong male figure I was ever exposed to.

Grandma and Grandpa Thomas were an odd couple. He was a kind, gentle, incredibly pussy-whipped man, and she was a neurotic, fiercely loyal tyrant. They took great joy in their Polish roots, which added to my fascination with them. They managed to raise five children in a two bedroom house, and, as adults, none of them moved more than a few blocks away. Every Sunday the entire family, which now numbered around thirty people, would come over for stuffed cabbage or smoked shoulder. Grandpa did most of the cooking, and he made the best mashed potatoes ever. Grandma had endured a violent and rocky childhood, and she wore her bitterness like a war medal. Somehow it made her edgy and charming to me, though. I credit her with instilling my germ phobia, as well as my devastating fear of being seen naked. Yup... I was so shy that I would not even undress in front of my mother... which is what makes my initial career choice all the more bizarre. I thank the Lord (although I miss her) that she died before she could impart any paralyzing sexual inhibitions. She, more than anyone, truly made me a jumble of dichotomies, and gave birth to my favorite mantra: "I'll lick your ass, but don't take a sip from my drink."

Being the eldest of three children from a broken home, I had to grow up quickly. In honesty, I feel like I skipped childhood altogether.

Until my parents split, I was being groomed for the ivy leagues, labeled a genius by some dumb tests, but that all went to hell when my unaffected father abandoned us in search of his own gratification. This was both a blessing and a curse, since he liked to grab us by the hair and smash our heads together when he was frustrated... which happened with increasing frequency towards the end.

My mother then poured herself into a lucrative real estate career, both to numb the pain from the breakup, and to dig us out of the debt that her husband had left us. Eventually she began dating again, trying desperately to find us a new father. This meant that she was always on the go. We barely ever saw her. I have come to learn and appreciate that she needed to find herself, but in doing so, she lost us.

My siblings and I were left to our own devices, with little guidance as to the proper path we should follow. Even though I graduated a year ahead of my high school class, college became a whimsical afterthought. Some days I regret not having pursued my early goal of becoming a lawyer, but my life has been a heck of a lot more interesting as a result.

These are the things that are racing through my mind like a near death experience as I squeeze my tits together to grasp a dollar bill from an admirer. It makes me laugh to think that anyone would pay me

10

to strip, because I frankly was not very good at it. Some girls are born naturally cunning and sexy. I was not one of them. I feel clumsy trying to be erotic, and just want to bust out laughing. I felt corny doing this, but it was the only way to stay in Florida. I hate the cold weather of the north, so I take a deep breath, bend over to grab my ankles, reach one hand between my legs, and simulate masturbation through my g-string. The crowd goes wild. I just giggle and listen to the crumpled bills being thrown on the stage. Thank goodness men have such simple needs.

My friend Libby and I had fallen in love with Daytona while we were camp counselors the previous summer. She was a chunky, animated Hispanic girl from Chicago that I met in college. Neither of us could stand another winter, so we packed up and headed south. Naively, we thought that since it was a tourist community, there would be plenty of jobs. We were incredibly wrong. We applied at every restaurant, gift shop, and gas station for miles, but no one needed us. We faced the reality that the only jobs available were as exotic dancers. Not exactly what we'd had in mind, but we were not quitters. We both were committed to staying in our new tropical oasis.

Our first endeavor with burlesque was a seedy bar on the outskirts of town called Pandora's Box. We went on amateur night, which is basically a strip joint job interview. You could have plucked this place straight out of a bad movie, it was so cliché. But, we made the best of it, donning our six inch heels and flesh tone pasties.

Libby went first. For a big girl, she really got a response from the patrons. This was lesson #1 in my education about men. Apparently, men don't mind a few extra pounds as long as you're slutty enough. She instinctively knew how to work the crowd, and made a wad of cash.

Then, it was my turn. Even though I looked pretty good, I just didn't have the same vibe, and the crowd didn't react as kindly. I made a few bucks, but they felt like sympathy votes. It was then that I realized that the flat stomach and big tits were not what the guys were paying for. They wanted to connect. They wanted to feel like they had a chance to take her home. It wasn't about eye candy; it was the fantasy that she was attainable.

Pandora's was way too skeevy to work at, but we had made it through the night with relative ease, and we resolved to find a better club. For me, a light bulb had gone off, and, however contrived it felt, I knew what I must do to succeed in my new world.

I quickly surveyed the crowd as I flipped my long brown hair back over my head. The ends gently stung my ass as they made contact. There were young guys with mullets, some impressive beer bellies, and a few old farts with ball caps displaying the numbers of their favorite drivers. An unassuming fellow with kind, happy eyes stood aside the stage with a handful of bills, which I stretched my garter to accept. Apparently, he liked what he saw.

My song ended and I put my bra and dress back on. He and a friend were sitting at the bar right by the stairs leading from the stage. Who would ever think that my good manners would shape the course of my future? I had to go thank the man.

I extended my hand and offered my appreciation. He said his name was Jack, and that his stocky companion was Rusty. They were in town for the races, representing one of the more successful drivers. Jack seemed disappointed that I was not a NASCAR fan, and therefore was not impressed by him.

They were both friendly and amusing. What they lacked in physical appeal, they made up for with charm… and, boy, were they working that angle. I had the feeling that they were not new at this. They were definitely looking for some action. Jack offered me $300 to go back to his hotel room with him, which took me less than a second to decline. I explained that I was not a hooker and that if he had simply asked me out for dinner I probably would have fucked him just for the hell of it. He apologized and tried to back peddle, but I wasn't having any of it. It had been too long of a night already, and I didn't have the patience for this familiar debate. Before I could make my escape, Libby, smelling an opportunity, had moved in on Rusty. The fat, ugly guys usually dropped a fair amount of cash if you feigned interest. It was the end of the evening, and she was squeezing him for all he was worth.

Before I knew it, Frank Sinatra was playing, signaling that it was time for our grand finale. All of the girls took the stage for a sloppy high kick lineup to the tune of NY, NY. The Rockettes would not be pleased.

We waved goodbye to the remaining pervs as the house lights rose, and scrambled up the steps to the dressing room. Libby informed me that she was going to party with Rusty, and that I had been volunteered as wingman. Fuck. That was the last thing I wanted to do; and, they weren't even cute. Apparently, they had some pot, and she wanted to get high. Being that she was the one with the car, I got roped into a lot of these situations... but she typically only went for hot guys with hot friends, so this one had me confused.

My pleas against this plan fell on deaf ears, and before I knew it, she was knocking on their door. They were even more repulsive in the harsh light of the Motel 6, or whatever crappy place they were staying. I silently promised myself that we would make this quick.

Rusty lit up a joint, and Lib began sucking it down. I had never seen her this way before. All of my friends knew that I didn't approve of drugs, so they generally kept them away from me. I was pissed, and decided that I would walk home. Jack reminded me that it was after 2 a.m., and that it wasn't safe to go alone. He admitted that he was still drunk, and shouldn't drive, but if I waited a while for him to sober up, he would give me a ride. Sensing that I was uncomfortable even being in the presence of the smoking, he coaxed me into another room.

How convenient... no place to sit except for the bed. It just kept getting better and better. Libby and I tried not to leave each other alone in potentially bad situations, which, in hindsight, would have been smarter than both of us having been there. Still, something told me that maybe this wasn't a complete mistake. I have always believed in fate and destiny, and now a little voice was telling me that this stranger was going to be the father of my children. "Impossible," I thought to myself. After all, this guy was not remotely my type, and I most definitely did not want to have any children. Not now, not ever.

He began making small talk, telling me about his home in Richmond, Virginia; how he was 42 years old, had a teenage son, and had been married three times, twice to the same woman. It all seemed a bit bizarre, but we were beginning to make a connection. I told him my story about getting into the "entertainment" industry, how I didn't intend to do it much longer, and that I had hoped to go back to school as soon as I could afford it. He seemed like a nice guy with a good heart... a poor schmuck who'd gotten the short end of the stick a few times. I'm a sucker for a sob story, so I bought it hook, line and sinker.

Even so, before long, I grew weary of the chit chat and decided it was time to go. I grabbed my purse and headed out the door to find Lib. I got a big eyeful of Rusty's hairy ass pounding away at my friend, who was now bent over the side of the couch. She swiped her arm as if to command me to go back in the room. I did, but kept the door slightly ajar so we could watch them go at it for a while. All of a sudden, things had gotten interesting. Even though neither of them was particularly attractive, fucking is fucking, and I was not going to pass up an opportunity to see some.

Sensing how horny I had gotten, Jack seized the moment and slipped his head under my skirt. He began lapping up the steamy juice that was welling in my panties. I was so engrossed in what I was witnessing, that I barely noticed that he was doing it. That is, until he made me cum.

I'm not going to say that I'm the kind of girl who would screw anyone, but I am the kind of girl who likes to get off, and once a guy's hot breath hits my cunt, I have no choice but to get fucked. He was in the right place at the right time, and I gave in to my mounting needs.

We fell back onto the bed, and without removing his face from my pussy, he slipped out of his pants. He ate me more enthusiastically that I'd ever been eaten before, and I rewarded him by creaming everywhere.

For me, oral sex and cock are kind of like peanut butter and jelly; one is just not the same without the other. They're each good, but you really need both for the full effect. I ordered him to give me his meat. He was one of the oldest men I'd ever been with, but it still surprised me when he needed a good deal of attention before we could slip a condom over his sagging package. Nothing seemed to work. It was like trying to get a Slinky to go *up* the stairs. Frustrated and annoyed, I told him not to worry about the wrapper, to just give me the goods. If he held it in just the right way he could kind of stick it in. It was late, and I didn't much care. With a little bit of friction, he eventually reached a solid state, and it wasn't half bad. I was particularly impressed when he pulled out and began going down on me again. We spent the next few hours sucking and fucking, and getting me off. He stroked his cock while I sat on his face, keeping it ready for action. I tried to keep the perfect balance of not giving a shit about him, but still making him think I was the best lay he'd ever have. Eventually he declared victory over his affliction when he pulled out of me and spunked all over the wall.

I'd worn the old man out, and he collapsed on top of me, snoring with delight. It was bad enough that I'd fucked this guy; I was under no circumstances going to cuddle up and savor the moment. I sloughed him off like a winter jacket, and put my clothes back on as quickly as I could find them.

Libby was unconscious on the couch, so I rifled through her bag looking for the keys. She heard me and woke up, begging for another hour of sleep. Fine, I was pretty tired, too. Reluctantly, I crawled back into bed with Jack, fully dressed including shoes, with one foot on the floor. It was my juvenile way of protesting the whole event. I didn't want him to wake up and think that I was willfully spending the night with him.

When I saw the sun begin to rise I demanded that we go. Lib and I snuck out without alerting the men.

The phone was ringing as we got back to our apartment. Since it was 6 am, I immediately realized that Libby had given them our number. That stupid bitch! It was Jack, wanting to make sure that we had made it home safely. He was disappointed that I had left in such a rush, and wanted to know if he could see me again. They were only in town one more night. With sarcastic regret, I explained that it was a work night, and the only place he'd see me would be on stage. As I hung up the phone I heard him saying that he'd see me there. Oh, joy.

I took a scalding shower and hopped into bed, trying to pretend the whole night never happened.

Much to my surprise, when my alarm went off at 5 pm I awoke with a slightly different feeling. Maybe this guy was different. Maybe he was mature enough to appreciate my quirky nuances, unlike the other boys I'd been screwing with. There was also a certain discontent brewing inside me. While I was enjoying the power of playing the ice queen dominatrix whore, I was also longing for the comfort of home, family, and people who really loved me. Perhaps I'd explore this further. I would at least put him through my gauntlet to see whether or not he could be scared away. No one had survived it so far. Nothing makes a man run faster than a free spirited, sexually aggressive girl without fear or boundaries, and an obsession for shock value. They had to accept that part of my personality before I would begin to share the softer, more vulnerable side. My secret was safe. None of them would ever have guessed what a kind-hearted, insecure, submissive girl I really was. I had almost forgotten myself.

Chapter 2

Just another day on the job…

The line was out the door when we arrived at the club. Jennifer, our transsexual hairdresser was slapping girls' faces on, dousing them in Aquanet, and practically pushing them down the stairs to meet the demands of the rowdy bunch. I felt like a sheep being thrown into the lion's den, but it was probably the other way around.

Smoke and testosterone hung like a thick cloud over the restless sea of glassy eyed men. They were packed like veal tonight. Cha ching. It was the last night of race week, and by the end of the evening there would not be a single man in Daytona with a dollar bill in his pocket.

As I strolled the floor in search of my first conquest for the night, a hand wrapped around my wrist, pulling me backwards. These guys had started drinking early. It was a beefy, curly headed kid who barely looked old enough to be there. He wanted a lap dance, so I took him to a dark corner and sat him down. He presented me with a hundred dollar bill, and told me to keep the change. I always wondered why men who looked capable of getting a free piece of ass would want to come here. As I straddled his knee, I couldn't help but ask him. He told me that most women didn't understand him, and that he felt more comfortable talking to dancers. I accepted his explanation, and went about my business. I knew he was enjoying it, because I had to keep removing his hands from my panties. Some of these girls allowed big spenders to take liberties when the bouncers weren't watching, but he had chosen the wrong chick. He obviously lacked social skills and manners, which is likely why he was now paying for this attention. Mystery solved, because I certainly would not have tolerated his advances for a dinner at Red Lobster. The song ended, and I was getting ready to leave when he pulled out another hundred. We negotiated that he would keep his hands to himself if I would stay for one more dance. This time he wanted me to face the crowd so he could watch from behind as I hovered over his lap, bouncing and writhing as if he were inside me. I was distracted, wondering whether or not Jack would show up. While I was bent over I searched the room for him. Much to my surprise, there he was, up in the champagne section. I hadn't seen him come in. My focus abruptly reverted to the task at hand when I felt a warm jet of goo hit the small of my back. Dance over. I wiped myself with a damp cocktail napkin, motioned for security, and away he went, dragged swiftly by his collar. Most girls would have been freaked out. I took it as a compliment.

After a bit of freshening up, and a quick costume change, I went to where Jack and Rusty were sitting, several of my coworkers on their laps, guzzling Dom Perignon. Sammy, an older, leggy blonde, with tits the size of cantaloupes, which could be seen from behind her slender frame when she raised her arms, jumped up when she saw me. Apparently, she had been told that he was there exclusively for me. I thanked her for keeping him warm, and she left to take her turn on stage. Jack apologized for not being alone, but it was unnecessary. I know these girls; they're like vultures, especially when booze is involved. He offered me a flute of champagne, forgetting that I was not yet of legal drinking age. No one would have stopped me, but I preferred to stay sober.

Libby was enjoying her first stint as our waitress, having finally paid her dues as a dancer. Oddly enough, their outfits were more revealing than ours, yet still remained within the law. I ordered a sparkling water, and she sauntered off to get it, steaming mad that Rusty was getting continuous dances from her rival, Lisa. Although strikingly gorgeous from a distance, up close, Lisa was a shriveled crack whore with the fangs of a vampire and absolutely no tits. She was funny, though, and a 20 year veteran who really knew her moves. She and her boyfriend had been trying to get me in the sack since day one. I regret not having had the balls to take them up on it. She was probably hot in bed, but I was certain that she had to have some form of something incurable. It was one of my fleeting moments of sound judgment.

The night flew by as we laughed and got to know each other. When I went on stage he filled my garter with ones, and when my performance was over I went right back and sat with him. Not a good decision from a cash flow standpoint, but I was having fun.

It was getting late, and almost time for our final goodbye, when he offered to stay an extra night if I'd join him for dinner tomorrow. What the heck. I agreed, and headed for the stage. When my name was called, he hooted and hollered, and stuffed a few more bucks down my stockings before the bouncers made everyone clear out.

On the drive home I told Libby that I'd probably lost a lot of money by sitting with them and not working the crowd. She smiled, threw some twenties at me, and told me not to worry. They'd been so drunk and preoccupied that when they signed their tab they didn't notice that she'd switched their $50 tip to $500. I couldn't believe it. I didn't know whether to be mad or proud of her. Now I knew why she always had so much more money than I did.

Sometimes after work we were all revved up, and knew that trying to get to sleep would be futile. One of our favorite late night activities was fucking with the cashiers at the 7-11 next to our apartment. They were usually bored, too, so it was almost an act of kindness. Lib and I were both enjoying our second wind, so we wandered across the street to check in on our nocturnal buddies. There was only one on duty tonight. His name was Bruce. He was a tall, physically unappealing man with a skin problem, most likely in his mid forties. We guessed that he was probably still a virgin by the way he nervously giggled when we spoke to him. We told him graphic fictional stories about how we were lesbians… what we'd just been doing to each other, and how we'd love to get him in the mix sometime. His left hand had been down his pants since we walked in, and we made a game of trying to get him to show us what he was holding, but he would not oblige. So, as an extra incentive, Lib flashed him her boobs. It made her hot because she knew that the security cameras were on. We were all having a good time, and I think he was finally about to whip it out, when the store manager showed up. She was not quite as friendly, so we decided to move on to plan B: Denny's!

Now, I'm not exactly sure where Lib got the notion that a woman should never have to pay for her own meal, but she firmly believed it, and was not shy about roping strange men into picking up our tabs. I usually hid in terror, wanting to crawl out of my skin, while she was working her magic. It was completely embarrassing, but she always knew just what to say, and she never failed. Her theory was that men enjoy doing things for women, and needed only to be asked. Tonight was no exception. Where had she gotten these balls, and why hadn't I ever grown any? In spite of the fact that it was 3 a.m., she had no problem waking Jack up out of a dead sleep and instructing him to meet us for coffee. He was groggy, but jumped at the chance to spend some time with us, especially intrigued when we told him that we were bringing a friend.

Denny's was like our second home. We knew almost everyone there and even had our own special waitress. Her name was Susan, but we called her Prego, because she was about to pop her third child. She tolerated and generally enjoyed our antics, so we tipped her well, and she looked forward to our visits.

Jack was waiting for us in the parking lot when we arrived. He was blissfully unaware that this was a test. I was eager to see how he would react to our friend, Kitty. My heart fluttered when he shook her hand and introduced himself. Kitty didn't reciprocate the niceties, because she was my scantily clad blow up doll. Without batting a lash, he took one of her arms and escorted her into the restaurant, asking the puzzled hostess to seat us at a table for four. "In Susan's section," I added.

We tied Kitty to the chair with a bungee cord, and pushed her in, just like she was a real person. Prego brought her a coffee, and Jack stuck a lit cigarette in her mouth. By this time, the drunks had consumed enough grease and pancakes to be sobering up, and a few of them had to look twice to figure out what was going on.

It didn't take long for the cops to pay us a visit. It was the only time Jack squirmed at all. He almost choked to death when I smacked the Sergeant on the ass. He didn't realize that they just wanted to say hello, and give Kitty a little peck on the cheek. We were a fixture, and no one minded our playful guest as long as it wasn't dinner time.

Seven coffees and three Grand Slams later, we called it a night. Prego was well trained, and knew exactly where to present the check. Libby taunted Jack into leaving an additional $10 on the table when he failed to put a sufficient amount on his credit card for her taste. I held my breath until the transaction was complete, fearing that Libby's switcharoo with the numbers earlier might cause his card to be declined. Luckily, it was not an issue.

We said goodbye, and Jack promised to pick me up at 6 for our date. He had impressed me, and I was actually looking forward to seeing him again. Even more amazing was the fact that Libby liked him. She never approved of anyone I dated. Her blessing should have been enough to make me run, but instead I viewed it as a sign that maybe the voices in my head were correct. Maybe he was the man I was supposed to marry. Nah, he was really ugly. I'd let him buy me dinner, but I couldn't get past the comb-over or the southern accent. That's where I had to draw the line.

Chapter 3

Our big date

It was no mistake that I was not home when Jack arrived to pick me up. There were two objectives to my tardiness. First, I needed some extra time to talk myself into actually sitting across a table from him, and second, I was curious as to just how long he'd be willing to wait. My general litmus test was that if a man stuck around for more than an hour, he had no respect for himself, and that's a huge turn-off, but if a guy didn't wait at least 30 minutes, he didn't want me badly enough. Chicks should be more mature before God gives us our pussies. We have them from birth, and learn at a very young age that they give us license to torture men simply because we have one. He should stitch us up until we learn compassion and come to grips with the whole female power struggle thing. Maybe then men wouldn't have to make such assholes of themselves. Of course, God should withhold their penises until men are mature enough not to put their brains on autopilot, and let their cocks make their decisions, or to stick them in every warm, moist hole they find without thinking twice. On second thought, I guess we deserve each other.

I sat at my neighbor Brandon's apartment watching Jack through the window. Brandon and I had screwed around a few times. He was a sweet, super good looking, Iowa guy with a smoking hot weightlifter body. You've all seen movies where some Adonis lifts his bitch up and fucks her while he's standing, carrying her full weight, bouncing up and down on his pecker... but how many times have you actually done it? He was famous for it. If it were not for the fact that he was saintly and naïve, had a pencil for a prick, and liked to stick his finger up my ass while he was going down on me, I could almost have fallen for him. Heck, he let me hide out at his place to wait for another man. What does that say about him? In all honesty, though, I think I did let him eat me out while I was peeking through the window, so, it wasn't completely ridiculous of him to want me there after all...

At precisely 6:37 PM I saw Jack's brake lights go on, and I bolted out the door to stop him from leaving. He had waited an appropriate amount of time, so I deemed him worthy of my company for the evening. He was excited to see me, and was relieved that we were finally on our way. We were late for our reservations at the fanciest steak place on the beach. I explained that that was alright, because I was a vegetarian. His poor face dropped. Once again his efforts to impress me were failing. I was a trooper, though, and assured him that I'd find something on the menu to eat.

Unfortunately, the conversation was more interesting than the meal. I had a salad and French fries, while Jack wrestled with a rubbery piece of prime rib. I learned about all kinds of disgusting southern things, the most traumatic of which was "red-eye gravy." I swear I thought he was lying to me when he said it was made out of bacon grease and coffee. Who the fuck thought that one up? I was certain that this was a clear sign of inbreeding taking its toll.

Dinner had run its course, and it was time to figure out where to go next. He offered to take me dancing, since it was my favorite thing to do, but I nipped that one in the bud. There was no way in hell I was going to be seen in a bar with a "Hair Club for Men" drop out. I had a reputation to worry about. Or, more aptly put, I didn't want the other notches on my bedpost to see how low I was willing to stoop. That would have been insensitive.

Reluctantly, I agreed that we'd cut to the chase and go back to the motel. I'd had enough witty banter for one night. It was time to get some, even if it had to be from him. Plus, if we hurried things along I could fuck him, get dropped off at home, and go back out to the bars just in time for all the action. It was always nice to get laid before dancing, because that took the edge off. I could kill two birds with one stone. I'd thank him for dinner and relieve my tension all at once. The planets were aligning.

I was on a time sensitive mission. I needed to get off, blow his mind, and then talk him into letting me go home… pronto. Earlier that day I had gotten a bit experimental in the shower, and shaved off my entire bush. My twat was as silky as a baby's ass. That turned out to be my lucky charm. He thought he'd died and gone to heaven last time when I had a small runway. Seeing me bald made even his limp sausage into hard salami. Thank God! Licky licky, bang bang... Houston, we have takeoff. I was out the door with his keys and a big sense of accomplishment before he could get his jeans back on.

I felt like I was being followed by a big, creepy penguin as he waddled down the steps after me, pulling his pants up as he moved along. He was clearly disappointed that I wouldn't spend the night, and decided to head back to Virginia after he dropped me off, since he had lots of extra energy. I tried my best to act sorry, but I was never a very good liar.

Finally, we were back at my place. I was so close to freedom I could smell it. Then there was that uncomfortable moment where I knew he was going to want to make out. I had to hum the theme from Sesame Street in my head to keep from going insane while he gave me a dreadfully long, sloppy kiss goodnight. I think that's why I like giving head so much. It takes their minds off of wanting to put their tongues in my mouth. I'd so rather suck a dick than a slobbery, germ infested tongue. Kissing was never my thing, especially when I was forced to kiss toads like this one. And, regardless of how many I kissed, not one ever materialized into a prince. Damn fairytales....

Even though Jack and I had only spent a few nights together, it was the closest thing I'd had to a relationship in a while. It felt like a huge weight had been lifted from my shoulders when he phoned the next day from Virginia to tell me that he'd made it home. I felt more comfortable knowing that he was ten hours away. I could go back to being my naughty self. I had no intention of ever seeing him again, and

I set about putting as much emotional distance between us as I possibly could.

Chapter 4

What was I thinking?

Lib and I didn't own a coffee pot since they brewed it fresh once an hour next door. Talk about convenient! I decided to get a cup of mocha java to wake me up, so I dragged my tired ass over to 7-11. On my way home I noticed a yellow corvette poking along at a suspiciously slow pace. The driver seemed to be looking for something, so I asked if he needed help. It turned out that he was looking for me. The whole thing seemed strange, but that didn't stop me from engaging him in conversation. Apparently, one of the girls at the club had given him my address and told him to come talk to me. He had an offer that I shouldn't be able to refuse. He was a porn director from Miami named Jim who had been gaining a little bit of notoriety. He was in search of fresh, young talent. All I could see was a sexy man in a cool car, and it occurred to me that I sure could use a good fuck before I went to work. I invited him in for half a cup of coffee, and before either of us took a sip, we were screwing on my kitchen table. He had a massive stiff cock, which was a nice contrast to my recent digressions. It invigorated me to be taken in this way by someone so handsome, strong, and virile. Jack was the furthest thing from my mind, until the doorbell rang.

I wrapped a dishcloth around my bottom and answered the door. The delivery guy looked a bit shocked to see a topless woman standing in the archway. He turned bright red and got real sweaty as he handed me a vase full of roses. I asked him if he needed me to sign anything, but he just scurried away. Too bad, there was always room for one more.

My new friend bent me over the counter and penetrated me from behind while I read the tiny white card. It said, "I'm going to make you my wife. Love, Jack". I could feel the vomit welling in my throat as I tossed the note on the floor. The flowers were pretty, but they had come at an awkward time. I started fucking Jim with a renewed sense of determination, as if trying to challenge what I feared was my destiny... a life with an old, dried up, impotent, unattractive, biscuit eating southern hick. Still, the more I tried to resist it, the stronger his force felt, and the weaker I became to fight. I would tell myself "no," and a voice from within would scream "YES!"

Jim was also screaming "yes!" so I joined in. We ended up both climaxing together, and it was very intense.

Once we had caught our breath, Jim started getting down to business. I had passed the entrance exam with flying colors. He wanted me to come shoot some demo video for him. In exchange he would provide me with a furnished beachfront condo, a leased Mercedes, and a minimum of $5,000 a week directly deposited into my bank account. He said that I would work about three days a month.

Obviously, I would need some time to consider such an endeavor, so he would check in on me again tomorrow.

I must admit, it sounded tempting, and I gave it some serious thought. I was flattered by the offer, and imagined thumbing my nose at all of the people who had overlooked me in high school. I pictured myself driving up to the class reunion in the Mercedes, dripping with money and stories of glamorous parties and a cavalier lifestyle. I could see the waves crashing in my front yard, and could smell the leather seats. But, what would my mother and my grandparents say? They would be so disgraced and disappointed. They would never understand.

The mere thought that I would even entertain this lewd offer made me step back and question where I had gone and who I was becoming. There was a stranger looking back from the mirror, but I could feel the fat little girl who once aspired to be a nun, begging to be heard inside of me. She was ready to go home, and didn't like the new, morally bankrupt person that we had transformed into. Man, I had to shut that porky little bitch up. She was trying to ruin all of my fun!

The angel and the devil on my shoulders waged bloody combat as I got ready for work. It was becoming increasingly difficult to determine which one I was routing for. They both had strong arguments. I put on a tight red zipper front dress and headed off to the club.

There was a new stylist tonight; an actual woman. Not that Jennifer wasn't, but this one ovulated. She seemed like an odd replacement, because all she talked about the whole time she was making us up was how much God loves each of us, and how it was not too late to change our course. I'm sure the owners would not be pleased with her advice. She showed us pictures of her family, her house, her husband… all things that none of us really desired to have at the moment; perhaps with one exception.

As usual, I slid out of the chair looking like a Las Vegas showgirl reject, my hair too big, and my makeup too thick. They kept telling us that we looked good while on stage, but, up close we were a train wreck.

We all lined up in alphabetical order for our grand entrance: Bambi, Barbie, Candy, Diamond, Destiny, Ecstasy, Fantasy, Mercedes, Sammy, Sugaree, and rounding out the bunch, Vicki. I didn't feel the need to go by a pseudonym. The guys never believed it was my real name anyhow. Plus, it was easy to remember.

Tonight we started off with a "feature dance." We each wore a set of Pure Gold panties over our g-strings and sold them to the men as a souvenir with a lap dance. I friggin' hated having to do these. I just wasn't a hustler, and didn't want to spend the rest of the evening watching some drunken whacko sniffing my underwear. Since there were only 5 men in the place and 11 women to choose from, I managed to slip by unnoticed. I wasn't feeling very good, and my heart wasn't really in the game tonight. I went back to the dressing room and let the other ladies fight over the slim pickings.

It wasn't long before Anthony poked his head in to see if I was o.k. He and his brother, Franco owned the club. They were decidedly Italian, and there were constant whisperings of loose ties to the Mafia. Nothing excited me more! I always thought that I'd make a great Mafia Princess. Anthony was a robust 50 something guy with a jolly spirit, a cute New York accent, and a strange handlebar moustache. I was his favorite dancer, and he took me under his wing, but he was very shy around me. I think he knew that I wasn't quite like the other girls. I was more attracted to Franco, though, because he was tall and rugged, with an acne scarred face that made him look dangerous. He happened to be the only happily married man I'd ever meet in Florida, and I respected him for that.

For a long time I had wondered if Anthony was gay. He was timid and quiet, and became fidgety when I made advances towards him. My suspicions were put into question, though, one night after he'd had a few too many drinks. We went back to his home in a very nice gated golf course community. I was having visions of being the lady of the manor, recognizing a life that I felt sure I could grow accustomed to, when Anthony let it all hang out. He tied me to his brass bed, took all of his clothes off, and straddled my face, naked, dropping his balls into my mouth, while jumping up and down. I experienced a strange mixture of horror and amusement that night. It was like being molested by a hairy gorilla with rabies. It was quite dark, and I began to feel little pebbles falling into my eyes. I was mildly confused until he finished his little freak show and turned on the lights. I couldn't get out of there fast enough when I realized that what I was being pelted with were actually dried up dingleberries from his ass. Oh, my God… it was the grossest thing ever. We never spoke of it again.

I asked Anthony if I could take the night off, and he agreed to let me go since it was so slow. I thanked him with a hug, and began packing up to leave. Sensing my unrest, he offered to lend an ear if I felt the need. The people in the club had become like a family to me. Granted, it was a big, dysfunctional, incestuous family, but a family none the less.

Pretty much all of us had taken a turn with each other at some point. Not only did I have that "experience" with Anthony, but I actually dated one of the managers named Dave. I really, really liked him. He was sweet and soft spoken, and I could tell that he had a huge heart. It was no secret that he was in love with me, but I couldn't move past the constant odor of tooth decay and Crown Royal, so it was a short lived affair, even though I adored him otherwise.

Then there was Mick, the bartender. He was pompous, arrogant, conceited, and gorgeous beyond imagination. I didn't like him, but he was hot! Word was out that he was hung like an elephant, so I was always trying to get him to show me his cock. One night after work he walked me and Libby back to our car. He finally gave in and made a deal with me. He'd whip it out right then and there on the busy sidewalk if I'd suck it. I was always up for a challenge, and took the dare. It was all true… he was huge. I took the whole thing in my mouth right in plain view. People stared out the pizza parlor window at us in sheer fascination. At the time, I thought it was funny, but, looking back on it... well... I still think it's funny, but slightly embarrassing.

The night was still young, and my makeup was fresh, so it seemed pointless to go home. I decided to go across the street to Dazzles to do a little dancing. It was a pretty hip club, the hottest place to go for college age partiers, and it usually got hopping fairly early. Even at 8pm there was a line out the door. That wasn't a problem for me, though, because I was a V.I.P. I winked at the doorman and zipped past the line of plebes, into the myriad of black lights and pounding techno music.

Stefanos met me with a big smile. I hadn't seen him in a few days, and he had missed me. I considered him somewhat of a steady boyfriend, although it was no secret that he was married. He and his wife had an arrangement. She wasn't interested in having sex with him, so she looked past his transgressions, as long as they were discreet and respectful of her reputation. Her only stipulation was that her husband was not to embarrass her. Stefanos and I never were seen in public around Daytona. We would travel more than an hour to Orlando to go out for dinner so none of the wife's friends would accidentally bump into us. I was free to meet his sons, and many of his business acquaintances, but we couldn't go to the country club. That was fine with me, because he was just one of many, and I wouldn't have wanted any more from him than what he offered me. Since he owned Dazzles, I always bypassed the lines, never paid to get in, and all of my drinks were free. Plus, the sex was oddly exciting for me. He wasn't much to look at, a diminutive Greek man, well into his 60's, who could easily pass for the Grinch who stole Christmas, but he knew what he wanted, and wasn't afraid to ask for it. Truth be told, I learned a few important tricks from him that I still practice today. I think he recognized that I was more than a geisha, and wanted to see me live up to my potential. The best advice I got from him was never to wear cheap perfume. He said that if a woman smells cheap, she will be treated cheap. That one kind of resonated with me, and I immediately threw away my aerosol cans of musky stripper fragrance, and began wearing classier scents, even at work.

We slipped back to the privacy of his office, and began going through our ritual. He would hand me a napkin to remove my lipstick, so as not to mark him, and watch me slowly take it off. All the while he would be getting naked, folding his clothes in a neat pile. By the time I was done, he would be totally nude on his couch, knees bent and raised, exposing his tight little bum hole. He wanted me to start by tonguing his ass and sucking on his balls. Ordinarily I would not be compelled to do such a thing, but he was immaculately clean, and I felt comfortable with every part of his body. Plus, it taught me how much men really enjoy this, but are generally too afraid to ask, or don't know enough to, since they've never experienced it. I've ruined many men since then by employing this technique.

I would suck his cock for a while and then he would fuck me to get off, always using a condom, and always wrapping it up and disposing of the evidence in a special trashcan reserved for sexual refuse. I liked to peek in there to see how many lipstick laden napkins had been discarded before me. He was a very horny old man. Sometimes, towards the end of our relationship, his pucker would taste a tiny bit like spermicide, and I couldn't help but wonder if he was letting boys fuck him in the ass. It wouldn't surprise me, but I didn't really want to know.

When Stefanos had male friends visiting from out of town I would help entertain them. We would go to fancy restaurants where they would literally bring out every item on the menu, and then we'd go back to a hotel where I'd tag-team the men. One of them was supposedly the mayor of Athens or something. He gave me a set of silver worry beads that I still have today.

We would never leave the office at the same time. He would be back out in the crowd shaking hands and schmoozing by the time I reapplied my face, and regrouped enough to return to public. We would go about the rest of the night like strangers, each looking for our next conquest, neither of us bothered by the others' behavior. Stefanos and I understood each other. It was all about the sex, and we weren't ashamed of that.

Chapter 5

Let the good times roll

A few months earlier, I had been approached by a photographer named Keith Humphreys on the beach. He wanted to take some pictures of me, and we became friends. It turned out that his brother had actually been my photography professor in college. It is truly a small world. Keith and I had gotten together on several occasions to shoot some stuff, and, in exchange for being his model, he put together a portfolio for me.

Today he showed up at my door with some good news. He had entered my pictures in a contest, and I had been chosen as Miss Bike Week 1991. He said that I'd be in the big parade, and at the bike show. It sounded like a cool opportunity, and I was very excited.

On the day of the event, I wore a hand beaded black "bikini" which I had made out of a bra and panties, and thigh high leather boots. I hired Jennifer to do my hair, and she made me into a total trannie. I looked like a big haired man in his underwear. Still, it was an honor, so I sucked it up and Keith took me to the staging area. He had neglected to tell me that 2 other girls had also been chosen, but that didn't really bother me. We each wore sashes that showed our titles, which rotated between Miss Easy Rider, Miss Rat's Hole, and Miss Bike Week. We posed for pictures out in the freezing rain, and shivered our asses off. It felt more like Alaska than Florida, but it was still fun. I kept getting scolded by the cops for bending over too much, but that's what the guys wanted, and I aim to please.

I did some pictures for Harley Davidson, and ended up in Easy Rider Magazine. I never saw it, but I got phone calls from people I went to school with who had. That made it even sweeter. The best part of it all was that I had new bragging rights. It was the 50th anniversary of Bike Week, so it was a fairly big deal to have been a part of it, even though it wasn't as glamorous as I would have imagined.

Pure Gold was jam packed all week, and I was treated like a celebrity. My Aunt Cathy and Uncle Brad are big bikers, and they came down to visit and crash at my place. They even showed up to see me perform one night. It was strange stripping in front of my uncle, but I got over it, and he just melted into the crowd. From then on, I was royalty to them. We would walk around town during the day and people would want autographs and pictures with me. At one point we needed to cross a busy six lane street. They thought it would never happen, but by some strange twist of luck, I put my toe in the road and the traffic came to a complete halt, and we were able to cross. Now I was not just royalty, but a deity.

Cathy and Brad left just in time for my friends Chris ad Dwight to come down from Massachusetts. Now, when I say "friends," I mean that I knew them. Chris was my first boyfriend Pete's best friend. In actuality, we couldn't stand each other. I always felt like he tried to entice Pete to cheat on me, so I did my best to keep the two of them apart. In the end, Pete didn't need anyone egging him on to stray; he did it on his own. True to form, I exacted my revenge by fucking his best friend. Once Chris and I started screwing, we decided that we genuinely liked each other, and we dated for a while. Chris was only the second guy I'd ever had sex with. Vaginal intercourse, that is.

There was a small discrepancy regarding that point. Before I met Pete, I went out with a guy named Steve. Steve was the first guy I had oral sex with. He took me out on my first date and afterwards we went parking. He went down on me and then asked me to give him a blowjob. I barely knew what he was talking about, but I eventually got the hang of it. When he ejaculated in my mouth I rolled the window down and spit it out. Nobody ever told me that I was supposed to swallow it, and it didn't seem to matter to Steve.

We were really close friends, and hung out a lot together. One night Steve's parents were away, so he had a party. I brought my handcuffs and some body paint, and after Steve had a few drinks, we went up into his room to try out my toys. Things got a little heated, and next thing I knew, we were both naked. I figured that I wouldn't mind losing my virginity, so I didn't stop his advances. He was only two years older than me, and somewhat of an amateur, so it didn't go smoothly. It was very dark, and he was a bit drunk. I got the surprise of my life when he stuck his dick in my ass. I didn't know what to do. I thought he must have intended that, but I wasn't sure. A million things ran through my head. I didn't know whether to tell him, or just exactly what to do. I was really shy, and didn't want to look stupid. By the time I had made up my mind to say something, it was all over. I was confused but relieved. It was getting late, so Steve drove me home. I went to say goodnight to my mom, who was in bed, almost asleep. She asked me if I'd had a good time. I told her we drank, played poker, and then Steve fucked me up the ass. She thought I was being silly and said, "That's nice, honey…go to bed." I find that the more you speak the truth, the less people believe you. Anyway, in my mind, I was still a virgin, and told Pete that he was my first. Steve, however, bragged to Pete that he had fucked me, and it created a huge fight. The guys thought I was playing them, and I hated Steve for lying about having done me. It was really just a big childish misunderstanding. In retrospect, I prefer to think of Steve as having been my first. Pete doesn't deserve the honor.

I didn't speak to Steve for a long time, but eventually we put the whole thing behind us (no pun intended). We dated off and on for many years, and always kept in touch. He came to visit me 11 years later, and I finally worked up the courage to ask him if he knew what had happened that night. It turned out that he had no idea that I was a virgin, and, in fact, thought that I was quite experienced because of the way I spoke. He was horrified to know that he was my first. He said he never would have done it if he had known because it was too much responsibility. When I asked him why he stuck it in my ass, he replied, "I didn't know it was your ass, I just thought

46

that you had the tightest pussy I'd ever felt!" We laughed, and it remains one of my favorite stories to tell when I have a few drinks in me. Steve has been dead for several years now, but I still think about him nearly every day, and believe that he visits me in spirit on a regular basis.

Anyway, Chris had a girlfriend now, and didn't want to screw, which really pissed me off. He still wanted me to give him head, though, and didn't consider that cheating. I told him to go to hell, and I fucked Dwight instead. He had a big dick, and he was kind of cute, so it all worked out well.

When Chris and I had dated, I was just a waitress at Friendly's, so it was quite a switch for him to think of me as a stripper. My cool factor had gone up 1000%. Unfortunately, they were under age and couldn't come see the show. Still, I couldn't wait for them to go home and tell Pete about my amazing new life. I was glad that he would report that I had tons of men calling, that I was Miss Bike Week, and that I had fucked Dwight. It served him right. I needed him to see that two could play his game.

Dwight, Chris, and I were sitting around my apartment waiting for the clubs to open when Libby called from work, pissing her pants with excitement. Alec John Such, the original bass player, and one of the founding members of Bon Jovi, was in the club, and Libby was sitting with him. He had seen me at the bike show, and wanted to meet me. I didn't know who the fuck he was, and was no fan of 80's hair bands, but decided that it would be a fabulous thing for Chris to be able to report back home. Little old me, dating a rock star. Yeah, that certainly worked; and, at such a convenient time. I agreed to go meet him at Pure Gold, and left the boys to fend for themselves.

Lib was slobbering all over Alec when I arrived, but his attention shifted immediately to me. We chatted for a short time, but quickly ran out of things to say. He invited me to his room at the Marriott, and I accepted. He was with an Australian friend who was way hotter than him. The three of us headed for the hotel.

When we got up to his suite we hung out for a bit, and then Alec came up with a burning idea. He wanted to cut the crotch out of my pantyhose. He looked all around the room for something sharp, but couldn't find anything suitable. He remembered that he had a pocket knife down in his motorcycle, and he went to the garage to fetch it. The Australian dude and I made out while we were waiting for him.

Alec returned, and cut a hole, just as promised. (I kept those pantyhose for years as a groupie souvenir.) The three of us began a virtual fuckfest, and had a grand old time. I love being with two men at once. Alec had a Superman tattoo on one arm, and a scar from some surgery on his abdomen. I expected him to be a bit more exciting in the sack than he was, but his friend made up for it, and we all had fun.

When Libby's shift was over, she joined us. She was star struck by Alec. I couldn't care less about him. After a few more drinks, the friend left, and Lib and I had Alec all to ourselves. He wanted a threesome, and we agreed. We were so gay, though. Neither of us wanted to be naked in front of the other, and we got a wet washcloth to wipe his cock off after each of us had sucked it. I couldn't believe that Alec didn't just freak out and tell us to forget about it. It was the lamest night ever. He fell fast asleep when it was over, or, at least he pretended to. Libby started going through his closet and his toiletries, and I had to drag her out before she started stealing shit.

We went home and gloated to the boys, who were quite in awe of the whole situation. Mission accomplished! That was all I cared about. Alec called me the next day to have dinner with him, but didn't invite Libby. She was pissed and convinced me not to go. I can now say that I have stood up a rock star.

Chris and Dwight went back to the bleak New England cold, and I headed for the beach. I hated to have tan lines when I was on stage, so I came up with a plan to prevent them. I never wore a bikini bottom, just the thongs I wore at work, and instead of a bathing suit top, I sported some very small pasties. From a distance, I appeared topless. This served two purposes: a great tan, and lots of attention. It was a bold move for such an intrinsically shy girl. Occasionally, I would be approached by the cops, but no one ever gave me much trouble. I had almost forgotten the biggest benefit to the situation... families with small children immediately cleared the area, so I never had to deal with brats kicking sand on me. It was a perfect plan.

I caught a few rays, met a handful of guys, got some phone numbers, and hauled my stuff back across the street. Much to my dismay, there was a battered blue van sitting in my parking space. It was Jack; he had come to surprise me. Oh, fuck... more company... and terrible planning on his part.

I had hoped that my landlord, Mr. Hernandez, had not spotted the strange vehicle. He was certifiably insane, and kept us under very tight guidelines. He was a Cuban refugee who had made a lot of money in real estate, but ruled with an iron fist, and discounted the laws of America. He patrolled the street late into the night, shotgun in hand, always aimed and ready to fire on anyone suspicious. We were not allowed to have unrelated guests of the opposite sex after dark, and he would often walk into our apartments unannounced to make sure things were tidy, and that we weren't breaking any of his rules. Lib and I had to fib and pretend that we were waitresses, because he would never allow strippers to live in his building. We had to pay the rent in cash, and we were never to speak of him in public. Big Brother was always watching, but it did make me feel safer knowing that he had eyes in the back of his head, and an itchy trigger finger.

I pretended to be happy to see Jack, but he could tell that I was also a bit unprepared for such a "windfall of good fortune." This guy just would not quit. He said that he had missed me so much that he had jumped in the car early that morning, and had driven straight through. Ok, I was flattered, and appreciated the effort, but every time I saw him he just looked worse and worse. Had I been completely blind since birth, I would have instantly fallen in love... but my vision was alarmingly perfect, so my head was having a difficult time reconciling with my heart. He offered me the kind of love and attention that I longed for, but in a package that seemed like it was mismatched. I know that the old cliché talks about women wanting men who remind them of their fathers, but, my dad was a hottie, and this guy was nowhere near that. It did cross my mind, however, that since he was so completely repugnant to other women, he would have no choice but to be faithful. Maybe it could work to my advantage that he was a troll. After all, he did have some notable oral skills, and that goes a long way with me.

We sat in my kitchen and got caught up with each other. He asked me what I wanted to do, and I replied with the first thing that came to my mind. I told him that I wanted to go visit my family. An hour later, we were on the highway, headed to Massachusetts.

Jack got major points for spontaneity, and there's nothing I enjoyed more than a road trip. We talked and talked and talked, always having something to chat about, even if it was stupid. I tried to focus on his personality instead of the lack of physical chemistry, and, little by little, I could almost see myself with him.

Along the way, he brought me to the most fascinating place: Waffle House. I had never been anywhere so terrifying or magical in my whole life. It was as if someone had let all of the freaks out of the circus and taught them how to make omelets and hash browns. The women didn't have a full set of teeth between them, and the men were covered in tattoos and plagued by facial ticks. The place was packed with hungry rednecks, and the waitresses were shouting orders to the cook at lightening speed from across the room. Nothing was written down; the cook kept it all in her head and belted it out, all perfect, like she could do it in her sleep. I was immediately addicted. Back woods dinner theater at its finest.

I had to be brave and suspend my germ phobia, since they washed their dishes by hand, but that just added to the adrenaline rush. Everything ran like clockwork. Their HR department must have cornered the market on idiot savants, because no one in the place looked capable of having even a middle school education, but they were breakfast making robots.

My eyes were opening to the bigger world around me, and I liked being able to relax and to allow things not to have to be perfect all of the time. In a way, Jack was liberating me from myself. I felt comfortable and free, which was a testimony to his influence. I was falling for his soothing nature by the time we hit the Jersey Turnpike.

Chapter 6

Home sweet home

I called my mother from a phone booth outside a doughnut shop in the center of Shrewsbury, Massachusetts, and asked her what she was up to for the day. When she told me she was just cleaning the house, I told her I'd be right over. She laughed, of course, thinking once again that I was lying, and we hung up. Five minutes later I was walking through her front door. She didn't look half as shocked to see me, as she did when she saw Jack. He is slightly older than she is, and had not aged quite as gracefully.

The only person who hates surprises more than me is my mom. I guess you don't expect your daughter from Florida to just pop in unexpectedly, especially toting a geriatric patient, but she made the best of it, and tried to hide her panic.

Jack, true to form, was very charming and courteous, and managed to ingratiate himself. My sister, Becky, reluctantly gave us her room, making us promise that there would be no funny business in her bed.

Had it not been close to Easter, and had Jack not stuck a black jelly bean in my pussy, she would never have known what went on and she could have avoided an entire year of therapy. But, please be advised, jelly beans have a very low melting point, and they stain the crap out of flowery white sheets.

Jack and I made our rounds, visiting my dad and his side of the family, and everyone seemed to love him, once the initial shock wore off. I even brought him to meet some of my childhood friends, and no one had anything negative to say.

I had only known Jack for about a month, but he already was asking me to marry him. It was hardly the romantic moment I had dreamed about as a girl… it was more of a "hey, why don't we do it," sort of thing. He was testing the waters, I suppose. I kept telling him that I wasn't interested, but he kept bringing it up. It was like he was trying to brainwash me into thinking it was a good idea.

I expected my parents to freak out, but I guess they were trying to keep an open mind. They probably thought he'd set me straight, too, and they encouraged the relationship. I began to wonder if I was the only one who thought he was too old and too ugly for me. Everyone else put on a good game face.

One of my brother's friends, Annie Small, stopped by to see him while we were at my mom's. She and I had barely ever spoken at school, but we hit it off immediately this time. She was one of the craziest people I'd ever encountered. During her junior year of high school she had rammed her car into a moving train, and lived to tell about it.

Annie's tits were each easily as big as my head and her hair was wild, curly, and generally out of control. She had gaps between each of her teeth, and her eyes bugged out a little, but she was completely fabulous in her own way. She exuded an energy that is not often seen.

She was still living in Holden, where we had all grown up, and it was stifling her to the point of insanity. She begged me to take her with me when I went back to Florida. Hell, yeah; I could use a new partner in crime, and that way I wouldn't be alone in the car with Jack.

The next day, Annie, Jack, and I began our southward journey. We laughed our asses off the whole way back to Virginia. Ann was like an escaped convict, recently freed from death row. I was glad to help her, and I knew how she felt.

Jack kept hinting that he had a big surprise for me when we got back to his house. I was scared. Half of me hoped that he was formally going to propose, and the other half of me thought that I never wanted to see him again. Ann was certain that he was talking about an engagement ring. I didn't know what the hell to think.

Ten hours later, we pulled into the parking lot of Jack's rented townhouse. He was like a little kid, so excited to show me what he'd arranged. Before he could even get the key in the door, the smell of smoke nearly knocked me over. Once inside, Annie and I couldn't help but choke from the stale stench of tobacco. It was disgusting.

I was relieved, but under whelmed, when I saw a giant Easter basket on his kitchen counter. That was the big secret... he had sent his secretary out to get me an Easter basket, because it is one of my favorite holidays. It was far from what Ann and I anticipated, but at least we had chocolate for the ride home. Plus, it was thoughtful, and I did appreciate that he was trying to be romantic.

We spent the night in Virginia, and Jack rented us a car for the rest of the trip the next morning.

It felt good to be back on the road, and even better to be free from Jack once again. Ann and I entertained ourselves by taking turns flashing our tits at truck drivers. We were very popular all the way down 95. They must have spread the word over the CB that we were putting on a show, because, at one point we were completely surrounded by eighteen-wheelers. It was great!

I insisted that we take a little detour once we hit Jacksonville. I had been dating a guy named Jeff who was going to school in Ocala, studying to be an architect. We had met at Pure Gold one night a few months back and really hit it off. He was blonde and freckled, a little bit shy, but hot in the sack. I like him because he was so normal, raised on a cattle farm in Buffalo, NY. Tonight, he and his roommates were throwing a party, and I was not about to miss it.

Jeff was very excited when Ann and I knocked at his door. He greeted me with a big kiss, and handed us each a cocktail. We played some drinking games, hung out with his friends, danced, and totally let loose. Not unlike myself, Ann was a lightweight, and it only took a few beverages to knock her on her ass. Being a true gentleman, Jeff tucked her into his double king size bed so she could sleep it off. We continued partying, and eventually ended up in the bed ourselves. There was plenty of room.

Jeff and I began quietly making it under the blankets, trying not to wake Ann. God, I loved that boy. He had such a thick cock, it made me cum almost instantly. He was gentle but confidant, and our chemistry was undeniable. I was happy to snuggle up with him after it was all over. I felt safe and special just being near him. He was the kind of man that I would have married in a heartbeat, but, in the back of my mind I always felt like I wasn't good enough for him. I instinctively knew that he could never take me home to mom, and that made me kind of sad.

The next morning, Ann and I stumbled back out to the car, and headed for Daytona. I hinted around to see if Annie knew what had happened, if we had woken her up. Indeed we had, and, I was stunned when she revealed that she had been laying there watching us and masturbating the whole time. She had wanted to join in, but was too afraid to say anything. Bummer, because that would have been really hot.

Chapter 7

Last man standing

I couldn't wait to introduce Ann to Libby. We were going to be like the Three Musketeers; really tear up the town. Her Monte Carlo was in the driveway, but she was nowhere to be found. Ann and I unpacked the car, and it wasn't until I brought my bags into my room that I saw a note on my bed. Libby had deserted me and moved back to Chicago to be with her family without even saying goodbye. Apparently she didn't want me to talk her out of it. She stiffed me for that month's rent, and advised me to put the phone in my name. I could use her car until her dad was able to come get it, but it would only be about a week or so. She didn't think she could survive our environment anymore, and her parents had pressured her into making a fresh start back at home.

I was crushed. My mood went from glee to panic. How was I going to make it by myself? Our rent was high, and I was already struggling.

Ann bounded into the room with a big smile on her face. "Good news, there's a free bed now!" she exclaimed. Problem solved, she would be my new housemate. She would work with me at the strip joint, and everything would be a big party. Libby could go fuck herself.

I decided to take Annie to Dazzles. We were having a blast getting ready, just being silly. Ann had gotten two huge gum balls out of a machine earlier in the day, and she now had them in her shirt, like gigantic round nipples. Her tits were so big that they almost looked like they belonged there. Tears were running down our cheeks, we were laughing so hard. Best of all, she had the balls to go out in public like that. The guys thought she was hot as hell. Right in the middle of a conversation with a very handsome middle aged gentleman in a business suit, she decided to pull one out and start chewing on it. She gave me the other one, and I popped it in my mouth. The poor dude didn't know quite what to say. We walked away howling. It was so much fun fucking with people. I have never had such a good time in my entire life as when the two of us were together. She had a childlike innocence about her, even though she was perverted and insane. I allowed myself to let all of my guards down and just enjoy being young and free, which was a nice change of pace for me. My life had always been so heavy.

We partied until 6 AM, and she was still sleeping at 3 in the afternoon when I decided to go pick up a few things at the grocery store. I let her snooze, and went by myself.

Cereal, bread, Coke, and milk; those were the things on my list, but I ended up with something a little extra. Everyone says that the grocery store is a great place to meet men, and I proved that theory correct. I saw a good looking boy in the dairy aisle, and decided to talk to him. His name was John, and he was a college student who lived nearby. He was short and squatty, a little bit of a guido, but I imagined him having a thick member, so I invited him home.

Ann was still sleeping, so I tossed the groceries in the fridge, and John and I headed for my bedroom. He really knew what he was doing, and I had a hard time containing my pleasure. The construction of the building was so thin, I could hear my neighbor, Frank, in his apartment next door jacking off to my moaning. There wasn't even a solid wall between his bathroom and my bedroom, just a locked door. Sometimes we'd have entire conversations while he was sitting on the pot. Knowing that he was getting off made me even hotter, and more expressive, too. I came about 5 times.

I'm not sure how long Annie was standing in the doorway watching us before I noticed her. Had it been anyone else, I'd probably feel invaded, but I knew that she was loving it, and I invited her to come in. I was finished, so I let her have a turn with our new stud. She climbed on top, spread her legs, and rode him while I watched for a few minutes. Man, she had a big, hairy bush. I was going to have to help her with that! I left and closed the door behind me to give them a little privacy. About 15 minutes later, John emerged with a big smile, and a very spent look, declaring us the coolest girls he'd ever met. He was right... we were.

I immediately took Ann in the bathroom and shaved every bit of pubic hair from her crotch. If she was going to hang with me, she needed a bald pussy.

The next day I had to go buy a car. Lib's dad was coming for hers, and I would no longer have a vehicle. I ended up with a sweet ass Mustang convertible, and, all of a sudden, Ann and I were even more dangerous.

We cruised up and down A1A with the top down, flirting with guys, honking, and picking up strangers, all with Kitty buckled into the back seat. It was glorious, until I arrived home to find a desperate message from my mother.

Apparently, Ann had neglected to inform her parents that she was moving to Florida, and they had filed a missing person report. They ordered her to get on the first plane out, and that was the abrupt end to our time together. They forbid her to talk to me ever again when they found out what we had been up to.

On the way back from the airport I saw a group of 6 guys in military garb hitch hiking. I stopped to pick them up, and they all squeezed in, holding Kitty on their laps.

They were Air Force boys, just back from a tour of duty in Iraq. Being that I am a very patriotic girl, I decided to show my appreciation for their dedicated service to our country by fucking each and every one of them. We went to their hotel room and I did them, one after the next, until the condoms ran out. After that I let the leftover guys eat my pussy and lick my ass, but would not consider letting them screw me without protection. I tried to be very careful, even when I was being extremely reckless.

I had dulled the pain from the loss of my friend, and I felt a little better. God bless America, and our fine military.

Chapter 8

Happy birthday to me?

The phone started ringing early on the morning of April 11th, 1991. My mother, my brother, my dad, my sister… everyone was calling to wish me a happy 20th birthday. It was sweet that they thought of me, but I could really have used the extra sleep. I had worked the previous night, and the loud music still rang in my ears like an internal alarm clock. I was about to get a wakeup call, alright. Once again, I picked up the phone, wondering who was left that I had not yet spoken to. It was Jack. His voice sounded a bit eager.

"What's wrong?" I asked.

"Nothing," he replied. "Happy birthday!"

I could sense that there was something on his mind, and begged him to let me in on the secret. Finally he worked up the courage to ask me if I was having my period yet. I never really kept track of such things. It showed up when it showed up, and it wasn't a very big deal. And why was he so concerned with my menstrual cycle? I told him that I had not yet started, and that I wasn't sure when it was supposed to come.

"You're pregnant," he said, with every ounce of confidence that existed within him.

"Impossible," I replied, "I always use....." and there was a long pause as my whole life and every dream I had for the future flashed before my eyes. "Oh, my God... how did you know?" Jack claimed that he had a good memory for odd facts, such as when I was on the rag, and that he had counted the days. I ran to the bathroom to vomit. I'm not sure if it was nerves or morning sickness, but I puked my brains out.

I raced to CVS to buy a multipack of pregnancy tests, and hurried home to pee on each one of them. The directions said that results could take up to fifteen minutes to appear, but mine were instantaneous. Plus sign, plus sign, plus sign. Apparently I was quite knocked up.

Terror ripped through me as I began envisioning what this meant. I don't believe that there are any mistakes in life, so I was trying to be optimistic, but, for some reason, finding out in the way that I did made me even more frightened. I was having my own, private "Rosemary's Baby" moment. It was as if the devil himself had called me to let know that his plan was complete; like Jack had done this to me on purpose as part of his master scheme. He had instinctively and unequivocally known it even before I did. I felt framed, hunted, trapped.

I wept as I dialed his number. Jack was happy, ecstatic even. He started spewing out plans for our wedding, our future together; he had it all mapped out. He asked me to marry him once again, but I still had to decline. It was too much to process for one day. He offered to take full care of me if I'd be willing to move to Virginia. My head was spinning, and I couldn't commit to anything.

The next phone call was to my mother. She was floored, confounded, couldn't believe it; she tried to make me admit that I was joking. It wasn't exactly the love and support I had hoped for, but I can only imagine how disappointed she was for me. She told me to pack up and come home, and not to admit to Jack that he was the father, if indeed he really was. She thought I would be better off pretending I wasn't sure about paternity, so that no one would have any control over me. At the time I thought it was the worst, ugliest, most irrational advice I'd ever been given, to rob my child of its father... but, there have been many days since when I have regretted not listening. I felt more depressed and lonelier than ever when we hung up the phone. Plus, I knew that my mother has a really big mouth, and that within the hour every single member of the family would know my business. I decided to call and give them the news myself.

Grandma Christie was always glad to hear from me. I called her about three times a week, just to listen to her voice. She immediately knew that I was in trouble because I could no longer hold back the tears as I said hello. I thought that she was going to be mortified. I was so afraid of disgracing her. Instead, she beamed with excitement. She congratulated me. She couldn't wait to be a great grandmother for the first time. I had made her day, and she had made mine. I had been so worried about how she would react, that it never occurred to me that this might be a positive announcement. "Your children are your jewels," she said, "You are finally going to have jewels. This child will be your greatest blessing." Nothing since has ever been so true or accurate. Suddenly, I was able to allow myself to be happy and hopeful, but I was still confused about what to do.

Having grown up in the ultra-liberal north east, my immediate thought was to go to Planned Parenthood to get an official test, and to talk to someone about what my next steps should be. I figured that maybe a stranger could help me sort things out without inserting an agenda.

It took me a while to find the obscure location, but finally I got there. I filled out some forms, they took a urine sample, and eventually ushered me into a small, dark office to discuss the results. The counselor confirmed that I was expecting, and wrote an address down on a scrap of paper. She wished me luck, and told me to keep in touch.

"What's this?" I asked her.

"It's the location of the abortion clinic," she responded," in a matter-of-fact tone.

The timid part of me thought I should just follow her instructions, but almost immediately something welled up from deep inside of me, and I became enraged with anger. "Who ever said I wanted an abortion? I came here for some counseling. I just want to know which way I should go regarding the father!"

"Oh," she said, not even remorseful. "You are so young and so pretty, I just assumed that you were here to terminate."

Having an abortion never crossed my mind. It was never an option. So many things needed to fall into place for that egg to get fertilized. I knew that this was the path that God had intended, and I was not going to assert my own selfish wishes against His plan.

I sat back down and told the woman my whole story. We ended up agreeing that it would be in the best interest of the child to grow up with both parents. I decided that I would go live with Jack, but that I was not ready for marriage.

This was the day that I became a conservative. Had I not spoken up, they would have sucked my child out of me without ever presenting another option. It breaks my heart to think of how many women have been in my shoes; scared, confused, and just taking the first option presented. We should have at least talked about adoption, or what kind of help would be available if I chose to keep the baby and needed assistance. How do those people sleep at night? Why wouldn't they want the baby to live if at all possible? I was crushed and disenfranchised.

Pure Gold was my next stop. I quit my job and said goodbye to everyone. They wished me well, and said they'd miss me, but I was sure that I'd eventually see them again.

I gave notice on my apartment, and immediately started packing. Jack couldn't contain himself when he found out that I'd decided to move in with him. Once again, he asked if I'd like to get married, and once again, I declined. He told me that he'd add me to his health insurance, and start looking for an OBGYN. It was settled, I'd leave on the 15th.

There were a lot of men to call. Each one of them was sorry to hear that I'd be going, but relieved to find out that I was not pinning them as the father.

Everything I owned fit snugly in my Mustang. As I locked the door to my apartment and returned the keys to Mr. Hernandez, I closed that chapter of my life for good. Well, almost... I was still going to stop and visit Jeff for one last roll in the hay. After all, I was pregnant, not dead.

Chapter 9

Virginia is for lovers?

As I cleared the tollbooth welcoming me to my new world in Virginia, I realized that my life as I had known it was over. No more one night stands, dancing for money, or blowing old men in the back room of a club. It was time to become an adult. Soon, I would be a mother, and I intended to embrace that role as proficiently as I knew how... which wasn't saying much. I never had the strongest maternal instincts, and what I did have was systematically crushed by years of being told that I was a hard nosed bitch, meant only for business, and that I should never have a family. I felt certain that I could prove them all wrong, and I was excited about turning a new leaf. It would be comforting to wake up next to the same man each morning, and to know that he was exclusively mine, and I his. Maybe this was my chance at the "Leave It to Beaver" lifestyle that had so swiftly eluded me in my own childhood.

It gave me a false sense of comfort that Jack was older and had been through this all before. I would defer to his judgment, since he was such an expert. It wasn't as if challenging him was even worth while. Everything he said or did was right, and that was never open to negotiation.

Jack was waiting for me on his front stoop when I pulled up. He was wearing a flimsy pair of gym shorts, and a tee shirt with a pocket for his cigarettes. Had it not been for the intense glow of excitement in his eyes, I would have backed the car up and returned to Florida, because this was certainly not how I had pictured my future. Still, he was committed to making the best of our situation, and, to a degree, I thought it was worth a try.

We unpacked the Mustang and put all of my things in the spare bedroom. I ran to the bathroom to vomit, once again, not knowing if it was my nerves or the pregnancy causing the emission. Jack was gentle and concerned, and tucked me immediately into bed before brewing me a cup of warm tea. It was wonderful to be in the care of someone who loved me so much, and I became optimistic that this was a smart move. I snuggled in and was drifting out of consciousness when I noticed a small photo jammed in the corner of his dresser mirror. I got up to examine it, as if the picture had beckoned me to learn more. It was a forty-something blonde woman, rather attractive, but a bit hard in the face. I took it into the kitchen where Jack was washing dishes, and demanded an explanation. He nonchalantly told me that her name was Bobbi, and that she was his ex girlfriend, and that they were still very close, although their breakup had been a tad rocky. He told me not to worry, and that I should get some rest.

Eventually, he came to bed, and we made love as best we could considering his "circumstance."

He tried to cuddle afterwards, but I told him it was more comfortable if he kept to himself while I was in this condition. He honored my request, and we rolled to our respective sides of the bed. I stared at the blank wall for many hours that night questioning this relationship… realizing that I knew nothing about the man who was now the father of my child.

I awoke the next morning to the aroma of toasted bread and stale cigarettes. Jack had heard me tossing in bed, and had prepared breakfast for me. He ushered me to the big, comfy recliner, wrapped me in a blanket, and set me up with a tray table in front of the television. I was not a coffee drinker, so he had fixed tea, a peanut butter English muffin, and fresh cut strawberries. Never in my life had someone taken such good care of me. I could see myself getting used to this.

It was moments like these that made me feel a little crazy. I was constantly at odds with myself. To look at him, I wanted to run, but to feel his love, I needed to stay. It was surreal and terrifying. My wildest dream of admiration and acceptance, with my biggest nightmare of an oddly shaped southern hick with the thickest accent I'd ever heard. I burst into tears, not knowing if they were for joy or despair, but it was probably both, combined with a healthy dose of frustration. Part of me really loved this man, but the other part was scared to death, like I was trapped in some emotional haunted house, where the only way to get out is to plow through, and hope that there is daylight at the end.

I figured that a nice, hot shower was the ticket to regaining my composure. I turned the water on and let it run for a while, surveying my growing body in the mirror. I was beginning to show, even at this early stage.

I had not gotten three toes into the tub before I noticed a disposable razor sitting near the soap. My mind raced. I knew immediately that there had been a woman in that shower. I felt sick again, and threw up down the drain. I tapped the razor against the wall to empty its contents. Short, coarse hair splattered in clumps on the tile. Some bitch had been in Jack's shower, and I knew exactly who it was... Bobbi. Now, I am not such a hypocrite that I was jealous... after all, I had been with another man mere days ago, but it seemed strange that this guy who proposed to me on a daily basis had been screwing his ex girlfriend the entire time we'd been together. It made me wonder who I was dealing with, and if his dedication to me was as genuine as he professed. I didn't confront him, knowing he would make up some dumb story to explain it, but I tucked it away in the back of my mind. Jack was such a stranger to me.

In time Jack had to get back to reality and run his business. There wasn't much for me to do except sit and grow more pregnant. My life became one long series of talk shows and soap operas. My ass was beginning to leave in imprint on the recliner. Every morning when Jack left for work he would remind me not to open the door for anyone, especially, he said, a woman. Who was I, Snow White? That seemed like odd advice, but I took it at face value, not being completely aware of my surroundings, even though they seemed harmless. He gave me strict orders not to step outside or even get the mail. I was a prisoner in a dingy apartment for 8 hours a day. He forbid me to open the curtains or answer the phone unless the caller ID showed that it was my family. At that point I was too emotionally drained by my predicament to realize that something fishy was going on. I was nagged by the uncomfortable notion that Jack was hiding his true self from me. Sometimes while he was gone I would rummage through his drawers, cabinets, closets, and coat pockets, trying to gain insight as to who this man really was. One day I found a baggie full of pot, and I was pissed! He had sworn up and down that he didn't do drugs, but, there it was, ready and waiting. For me, it was proof that I didn't have all the pieces of this puzzle.

By the time 6pm rolled around I was desperate for human contact. I was bored and lonely, and he was like my savior coming home to rescue me. I would run to the door like a puppy when I heard the key turn. In a matter of days, my life had gone from that of a carefree, popular showgirl to a caged animal.

After a few weeks I could stand no more. I demanded that I at least be able to go work in Jack's store with him. He had a shop where he sold racing tee shirts, hats, memorabilia and collectibles. His patrons didn't exactly offer stimulating conversation, but I was happy just to be amongst people again. I quickly learned about all of the drivers, and soon I was knowledgeable enough to sound as if I belonged there; minus the southern accent, of course.

When there were no customers in the store we would often sneak into the back room and have oral sex. Sometimes his blood flow would cooperate and we could fuck, but at minimum he would eat me out.

Jack always had to have a drink in his hand, so he would leave me in charge of the store and walk to the 7-11 two doors down. The minute he was out of sight I went directly to the caller ID. It seems that Bobbi would call over and over and over again, even in the middle of the night. That didn't make me feel very good, and neither did the occasions when he'd answer the phone and then slip away to speak privately. Some days he would tell me that it wasn't convenient for me to go to work with him, and, by asking his son enough of the right questions afterward; I would surreptitiously find out that he'd had lunch with Bobbi. That pissed me off, and I made my feelings known. At that point Jack decided to come clean. Bobbi had a violent streak and a drug problem. They had broken up on Christmas Eve when the cops had to drag her from his apartment in handcuffs, AND she had done time in prison for the attempted manslaughter of another woman Jack had briefly dated. He was supposedly trying to pacify her so she wouldn't come after me. He was afraid that she would show up at our door and kill me if she found out that I was carrying his child. Nice... I swear there is nothing more insulting than knowing that your man has been perfectly content with trailer trash. It makes you feel like that must be all you are if that's what they're attracted to. Anyone looking at us would realize that I was out of Jack's league, just by virtue of the fact that I had a whole set of teeth, but this little epiphany really hit home. Jack was used to living and thinking in the gutter, and he was climbing up my back to get out. I knew that I was making a big mistake, selling myself short, but it was the first time that a man had ever provided for or protected me, so I tried to focus on the positive.

My greatest lapses in judgment came while Jack had his face between my legs. At those moments I would do anything for him. Logic didn't hold a candle to the way he could make me cum, and I think he caught on early and used that to his advantage. It was with a very creamy chin that he asked me once again to marry him. In spite of all the evidence I now had that this man was a piece of shit, I finally said yes. I am not very proud to admit that my first marriage was a direct result of little more than some good head and the teeny tiny fact that I was knocked up.

Chapter 10

The nine day engagement

Jack was elated when I finally broke down and agreed to be his fourth wife. Ah, what an honor. His first had been a high school sweetheart, and was long gone, his second, Sandy, lived nearby, and warned me that I was making the biggest mistake of my life. I couldn't really trust her advice, though, since she had a teenage son with him, and had married him twice. How bad could he be if she went back for more?

Like an impatient little boy, he jumped out of bed and insisted upon going out right then and there to purchase my engagement ring. We threw our clothes back on and headed for the mall.

I should have taken heed when the jeweler asked what the occasion was that my father was buying me a ring. We gingerly explained that we planned to be married, and he slumped away to compose himself. Again, I thought to myself, "Asshole... my dad's hot.... nothing like this loser!" Then I realized that maybe I should be embarrassed because even strangers could see that this was not a happy couple embarking upon a blissful life together; it was just a creepy old man and chick young enough to be his daughter.

I've never been a huge fan of jewelry, but I knew that I wanted something impressive to give me a sense of what a "catch" I'd made, so I opted for a ring of low quality but big wow factor. It had dozens of little tiered diamonds that almost looked flashy from a distance. After all, people would automatically assume that he was wealthy just by virtue of the fact that he'd snagged such a young babe. In his defense, Jack would have broken the bank, and offered many times to get a suitable ring, but I was too thrifty for my own good. My thought was that we had a baby on the way and didn't need to be wasting money on frivolous things. That was one of the areas where Jack and I definitely did not see eye to eye. He paid no attention to what he spent. Money was like water. I often wonder if it's because he actually believed he was well off, or if he was just putting on a show. I was hungry so I went to find something to eat while Jack paid for the ring.

We met back in the food court. Jack got down on one knee and presented the ring to me while asking for my hand in marriage. I said yes, and began to cry as he slipped it on my finger. They were not tears of joy, but rather droplets of disgust at the fact that the man I was going to be joined to for eternity had proposed to me over a Cinnabun. Fuck...what was I doing? Deep at the heart of the matter was a small tinge of shame that I would otherwise be an unwed mother. This was my way of legitimizing my child, even at the possible expense of my own happiness. I figured that I had experienced a lot of good times, and now I needed to sacrifice and think of the greater good, and what would be most suitable and proper for the baby. I was mature and juvenile in my thinking all at the same time.

On the way home we started discussing possible dates for the wedding. It was June 1st, and Jack had to take his show back on the road starting June 12th. Then, for the next 5 months he would be dragging from racetrack to racetrack with very little down time in between. We thought about waiting, but by the time race season was over I would be about to burst. Brides with huge bellies were not yet in vogue, and I didn't want to be the one to start that trend in my family, so we decided that time was of the essence, and we settled on June 10th. My entire family was living in Massachusetts, so it only seemed fitting that we would wed there.

The first call was to my mother. She was shocked to learn that not only had I gotten engaged, but the date was rapidly approaching. I could hear the disappointment in her voice, but it was too late to turn back now. I had made up my mind, and mentally prepared myself for what I feared might be a huge but necessary mistake. Jack knew that he could not sexually satisfy me for long, that after a while I would need a good hard cock, and the instances that he could provide that were few and far between. He vowed that if I ever felt the need to take another lover he would not stand in my way, and he would accept that it was merely a matter of primal needs, and not a slight to our relationship. I assured him that I couldn't foresee that happening, but thanked him for being realistic about the possibility. I intended to be faithful regardless of my passion for carnal relations, which was now made easier to stomach knowing that

I could always break the glass on that promise in case of emergency. We only want that which we think we cannot have.

I dialed all night long until the important people had been informed of our plans. Bridesmaids and groomsmen were in place within hours. I decided to walk down the aisle alone since my father had not been a positive or healthy part of my life up to that point. It would have seemed untrue to my spirit to allow him that honor when he had quite clearly shirked his responsibilities regarding us children. I wanted him there, but only as a bystander and captive witness to what my life had become as an indirect result of his absence. My mother still harbored strong ill feelings toward him and his entire family for the way everyone treated her when they split, and how none of them encouraged my father to support us in any way. She forbid me to invite any of them since she would be footing the bill and hosting the wedding at her home. I took a stand, though, and told her that she would not be invited either if she could not make amends for one day in order to facilitate a peaceful gathering. It was not that I didn't want to have a relationship with my father; he had just never offered one. I vainly hoped that maybe this would be a fresh start for us.

As the day approached, I made my way home to help prepare. Jack would fly up later. We had taken care of the blood tests and the marriage license, and now it was just a matter of the fun details.

Luckily, prom season had just ended and the malls were full of clearance gowns. I was able to find a beautiful white dress right off the rack, and the bridesmaids stumbled upon what they needed almost immediately. The planets were aligning, and, for a moment, I was actually excited and optimistic. Things were far from perfect, but I was determined not only to make it work, but for our life together to flourish. I was secure in the fact that finally a man wanted to be with me exclusively for the rest of his life. He wanted to care for me and our child, and that was something previously foreign to my existence. I was thankful that my days as a stripper were over, and I fervently looked forward to being a plain, boring, stereotypical mommy and housewife. It was my chance to show the world that I was not damaged goods.

Jack and I were married on June 10th, 1991, as witnessed by most of my relatives and a smattering of childhood friends. My mother hosted a small reception for her side of the family, and when it was over, we went to my father's house to celebrate with his side of the family. It made me sad that we couldn't all rejoice together, but, as I had learned so often to do, I took what I could get, and was thankful for it.

We rolled into the Westborough Sheraton shortly after 11pm that night, both of us mentally and physically exhausted. Neither of us felt the need to consummate our union, and opted to crash instead. I should have recognized this as a dark harbinger, but I chose to ignore it. We screwed bright and early the next morning, but I still haven't gotten over the irony that I, of all people, didn't even get laid on my wedding night. What the hell??? That is so fucked up.

My new husband and I jumped in the car and headed for a brief "honeymoon" at some godforsaken shit-hole motel near the Pocono Motor Speedway.

I've blocked most of the traumatic details, but I do remember the horror on the faces of the other guests when I showed up to the pool in my fluorescent green thong bathing suit. My ass was on display in all of its glory, with only a trivial piece of floss to cover my crack. Probably a fashion no-no, but I was having trouble reconciling the fact that my body was rapidly transitioning from a work of art to a full scale disaster.

Chapter 11

Domestic bliss

Had I ever fantasized about growing up and joining the circus, my life would now have been complete. Jack and I spent months driving up and down the east coast following the Winston Cup schedule. Just when I thought I'd discovered the smallest, crappiest, most insignificant, hole in the wall town from hell, I would wake up in a new one. It was quite the eye opener in a lot of ways, and I was basically happy. Even though we stayed in worn down motels and ate at grungy diners, or from vending trailers, we were together, and we got along exceedingly well. I loved feeling like I was a part of this big traveling hillbilly show, and enjoyed the fact that we were never in the same place for more than a few days. It was an exotic lifestyle, but in a plebian way.

I was getting to know Jack better, and liking 99% of what I saw. I felt lucky and blessed that I had followed my instincts and that I had not foolishly turned away from this man who adored me so much. We talked for hours on end, and I really began to develop a genuine soft spot for the challenges he had faced, and the hardships he had been through. We took good care of each other in a way foreign to both of us, and it really cemented the bond we now shared. It seemed like each of us filled the gaping void that the other once had. Any doubts or fears I ever conceived of were long gone. I felt bad about the way my mind worked when our relationship had started, and did everything I could to show my growing devotion. Both of us were ecstatic that we would soon have a child who would be a product of this profound love.

We had a few weeks after race season ended to prepare for our highly anticipated addition to the family. We moved into a fresh, clean, brand new apartment in a better part of town. It was nice to finally be in a place that wasn't haunted by Jack's past with Bobbi. It was ours together, and all of the memories would be started from scratch.

I was enormous, tired, and moving slowly, but we still managed to create a cozy nursery. We went to Lamaz classes, packed a suitcase, read the obligatory books, and did all of the gay things that expectant parents do. As it turned out, we could have taken our time, because this kid was quite comfortable right where she was. I wish I could have said the same for myself. I was anxious and severely uncomfortable. Finally, when I was 2 weeks overdue and quite obviously never going to go into labor, or dilate more than a few centimeters, the doctor agreed to perform a scheduled C-section for fear that the baby was getting too big. He projected that she could be as much as 13 pounds. Ouch!!!!!!!! I was thrilled that my pussy would stay intact, and that my junk would remain pristine and tight. It was like a dream come true.

My mother flew down from Boston so she could be there for the birth, and she went to the hospital with us on the morning of December 11th. I had never been sick, broken a bone, or even stung by a bee for that matter, so being in the hospital was a completely new experience for me. I was comforted by the fact that my mom was a nurse, and she eased my mind a great deal. Of course, I was so miserable at this point, they could have extracted the kid with pruning shears and a pair of pliers, and I would have thanked them.

I changed into a blue gown, got my identification bracelets, and was laid on a gurney. They wheeled me into a flowery little room, hooked me up to the IVs and the three of us waited for the anesthesiologist. Moments later a man in scrubs arrived to give me a local painkiller. So far, so good. He positioned me on my left side asked me if I was getting numb. Jack gasped and the blood drained from his face as I told the guy that I didn't think anything was working yet. The anesthesiologist disagreed and went about his business, leaving the room for a few minutes. Jack was trying to catch his breath and regain his composure, and my mother was giggling. Obviously, there was something they weren't telling me. When I got agitated enough Jack confessed that while the guy was asking me if I felt anything, he was jabbing a thick ten inch needle into my ass. He showed me with an erratic, exaggerated hand gesture just how big it had been. He said that the sight of the thing made him almost pass out, and he thought his knees were going to buckle beneath him. It creeped me out, but I was thankful that whatever the dude gave me was absolutely doing the trick. He returned to administer my epidural, which is one of the strangest, most terrifying episodes that I have ever been through. First they inject you between two of your vertebrae, causing an eerie, painful pop, which, for me, was horrifying. Then they inject something that causes a burning sensation in your spine. Luckily, you get over it quickly once the stuff takes effect. I swear that the epidural is by far the worst part about giving birth. Within moments I was loopy, smiling, and more than ready to get the show over with.

After what seemed like an eternity, the call came for Jack to suit up for the birth. I was brought into the operating room and draped to prevent me from viewing the procedure. They hooked me up to a bunch of monitors, and then the nurse pulled out a Gillette razor and advised me that she would be prepping the incision area. I was in la la land, so she could have shaved off my eyebrows and I wouldn't have said a thing. A moment later the nurse peeked around the covering and told me how delighted she was that I was already bald down there. She said I was lucky to have such a thoughtful husband that he would shave my pubic area. I told her that no such thing happened... that as big as my belly was, I still thought it was my duty to make that cooter sparkle. She turned bright red, and I never saw her again.

Eventually, Dr. Schaeffer waddled in, greeted me, and began cutting. I could feel tugging, pulling, a bit of pressure, and then I heard the healthy cries of our not so little baby girl. They measured and weighed her, wiped her up a bit, gave her an i.d. bracelet, and wrapped her in a soft blanket. I cried with joy as she was placed on my chest. I kissed her soft forehead and told her how much I loved her already, my sweet Alexis May. Jack held her for a moment before the nurses took her away for a proper cleaning. Jack couldn't control himself. He was sobbing and repeating himself over and over:

"Oh, honey, she's beautiful. She's just beautiful."

That was no understatement. Alexis was the most perfect creation I'd ever laid eyes on. I felt an immediate connection to her, and a love that cannot be described. I was so proud that I'd gotten through this, and that I had a gorgeous new person to love. It was torture being in the recovery room, waiting for the nurse to return her to me.

My mom came in and began supervising my care, making sure that everything was done properly. Once she felt satisfied that everyone knew what they were doing she started making phone calls. Becky and Jamie, Grandma Christie, Uncle David, and her boyfriend, Dane. I thought she might dial every number in the phonebook to tell them the good news. She was a grandmother!

Jack had been outside recounting everything to the small crowd that had gathered in the waiting room, and watching Alexis go through some more tests in the nursery through the thick glass. He was grinning from ear to ear when they finally allowed him to see me, and couldn't wait to tell me what went through his head in the delivery room.

Apparently Alexis was covered with a dark mucus when the pulled her from my womb. In his slurred twang he confessed that he experienced a moment of disbelief.

"You could've knocked me over with a feather when I first saw the child. She was as black as the damn ace of spades, and I thought to myself, 'Oh, Lord, Vicki's done fucked a nigger.' But I decided in that very moment that I didn't care. Even if I wasn't the father, I still wanted to raise her like my own."

After two nights in the hospital I was allowed to go home. It was wonderful to be back where I was comfortable and didn't feel like I was under a microscope. I could finally unwrap my package. The nurses kept Alexis so tightly bound in her blankets that I couldn't fully explore her. I marveled at the little fingers and toes, her sweet dimples, button nose, perfectly defined lips, and her thick black hair. We were all absolutely floored that she could already hold her head up. Babies don't usually do that for months. Perhaps she was later than we realized. My mother was there to guide me through the first days of uncertainty before she went home, but I instinctively knew what to do, and I had a hard time sharing the snuggle time. I held Alexis from the moment she woke up in the morning, all the way through her naps, and until she was ready for the crib when it was my bed time.

Sometimes I would watch her while she was sleeping and sob, worried that something would happen to her. One day I heard a voice from the heavens consoling me. It said "You ain't getting out of this that easy!" Strange advice, but it resonated with me. Nothing in my life had ever been simple. Here I was worried that the Lord would take my baby from me, when he was actually taunting me, reminding me that I had many, many years of hard work and sacrifice ahead of me. I needed to focus on that, and not the possibility that all of this new responsibility would be lifted. It gave me a bizarre sense of peace.

Things could not have gotten much better for me at this point in my life. I had a flawless little baby, a husband who loved me, and things we're going great. We drove to Massachusetts for Christmas, and to show off our new daughter. All of my family was there, and my brother had decorated the house better than Martha Stewart ever dreamed she could. He had given the tree a Chanel theme, and there were big, red bows everywhere. We enjoyed each other's company, and rejoiced that the family was expanding. For a moment I forgot that I had fucked up my life. It felt more like this should have been my plan all along, and that I had just taken a short side trip from my destiny. Being a mother and wife really agreed with me.

Jack showered me with lavish gifts and spared no expense to make me comfortable. Many times I questioned whether or not we should be spending our money so carelessly, but he assured me that he had it under control, that his business was thriving, but I couldn't help but notice that he was paying less and less attention to work, and more and more attention to us. In the same breath that he was calming my nerves he was begging my mother to loan him $12,000 for a new business venture. That was not cool with me, and sent up a big red flag in my otherwise pristine world.

I was so taken by the affinity I had for my daughter, our wonderful life together, and my doting husband, that I failed to be concerned about the fact that Jack hadn't gotten hard in ages. He would satisfy me and then roll over, but intercourse started becoming extinct. I tried to tell myself that I could handle it, that it didn't matter, but in the back of my head I was yearning for the days when I could experience the more physical side of love. Still, I couldn't complain. To a certain degree I had everything I ever dreamed of, and felt selfish to even consider that I might deserve more.

Chapter 12

Just shoot me

Race season started back up, and this time we were on the road as a trio. Logging 1000 miles a week isn't quite as much fun with an infant, but we made the best of the situation. Alexis was a very good natured baby, and she seemed to enjoy all of the attention she got when we brought her to the track.

Sometimes, when our work was done for the evening we'd hang out with the other vendors, especially the ones who stayed in their RVs on site. We tried to be particularly friendly with them so we could occasionally borrow their conveniences. It was no small blessing to use a clean bathroom, sit inside an air conditioned cabin, or watch television when the race was being run and business was slow.

We were in Talladega, Alabama on the night that "The Golden Girls" ended. It was my favorite show, and I just had to see the finale. It took some persuading, but eventually I found a couple who allowed me to hang out and watch it with them. I couldn't control my tears as Blanche, Rose, Dorothy, and Sophia said their goodbyes and the series ended. I was a bit embarrassed at how emotional I was. After all, it was just a dumb show, but somehow it really got the best of me that evening. I cried until my face was red and puffy. My nose ran and my eyes were bloodshot. To look at me you would have thought that my mother had been run over by a car or something, I was inconsolable. Then, like someone had clunked me over the head with a cast iron frying pan, it suddenly occurred to me: I wasn't sad about the show at all, it was my hormones, and I was fucking pregnant again. Now I really had something to cry about.

I didn't say anything to Jack; I just kept it to myself, hoping that my period would start and that it wouldn't be an issue. No such luck. A few days later when we were back in Richmond I slipped out to the store and bought a pregnancy test. I rushed to the bathroom inside Woolworth's and peed on the stick. That big pink plus sign didn't take 3 seconds to pop up and slap me in the face. Knocked up, once again! How could this have happened? I was truly distressed. Jack and I hadn't even screwed for months. It was almost as if it was an immaculate conception. I knew in my heart that I wasn't emotionally ready for another child. I had just given birth three months ago! The thought of taking any time away from Alexis really upset me, and I also had a sneaking suspicion that Jack was hiding our financial situation from me. The last thing I wanted to do was to bring another baby into the world. I felt everything crashing down around me. There were no good answers. For the first time in my life I actually contemplated having an abortion. I thought that if I didn't tell Jack, just snuck out and did it, that I could pretend this never happened and move on. My next thought was to buy a gun and go kill Dr. Schaeffer. I had begged him to tie my tubes after I had Alexis, but he refused since I was only 20. That man's life truly lay in the balance of my teetering sanity this particular afternoon.

I sat there and felt sorry for myself for a little while, but then a voice inside me insisted that I tell Jack. After all, it was his child too, and I didn't have the right to kill something that was half his.

Jack immediately knew that something was terribly wrong when he saw my face. I couldn't even speak; I just showed him the stick. He let out a very happy "yee haw" and began jumping up and down, hugging me. His happiness and enthusiasm got the best of me, and I never told him that I'd had an alternative plan. I knew I couldn't do it anyway, but it was such a delicious luxury to be able to contemplate it for a moment. I was jealous of the women who could justify that decision, knowing that I would never be able to put myself first. In retrospect, I am so thankful that the Lord prohibited me from that choice. Children are a gift, and I am glad that I didn't squander mine.

Once more I was dialing up everyone in my family to share the "good" news. I could tell by their delayed reactions that they all knew that this was not an ideal time to be having another child. Still, they feigned excitement, and tried to offer positive thoughts. It didn't ease my mind at all, though… I simply was not mentally or physically ready.

Jack decided that we should buy a house, so we began looking around for the perfect one. We both fell in love with a neighborhood called "King's Charter," and we contracted for our dream home to be built there. It looked like the ideal place to raise a family. It was full of young couples, and most of the mothers seemed to stay home with their kids, so I looked forward to finally having a social network. I was thrilled that Alexis would have friends to play with, and would have an opportunity to experience a traditional upbringing. I was all alone and isolated in our apartment. Everyone there was single, and it reminded me daily that my life was no longer my own.

Although I was quite sick from my pregnancy, I spent much of the next several months supervising construction, picking out light fixtures, toilets, cabinets, tile, and carpet. I designed the house to be unique and really represent my sense of style. I was so proud of how it was turning out. It gave me a great sense of accomplishment, and I was delighted to see it taking shape. Each week I sent video tapes and pictures of the progress home to Massachusetts so my friends and family could see what was going on.

It was about the same time that Jack really started pulling away from his business. It seemed like he never went to work anymore, and he would spend days at a time in bed. I really started to worry when I found out that he had let our medical insurance lapse. I tried to talk to him, and begged him to confide in me, but he kept insisting that everything was ok. I told him that I didn't need the house, that it wasn't important if we couldn't afford it, but every time we'd have one of those discussions he'd start making more elaborate plans, as if to convince me that he was solid.

As the months passed there were fewer and fewer deposits being made into our bank account, and I was starting to really get alarmed. Still, he encouraged me to plug away at the house, adding little extras every step of the way. He wasn't going on the road anymore, leaving that responsibility up to Rusty. I warned Jack that in a cash business he really needed to keep his thumb on things since it would be so simple to skim off of the top. He chided me for being ridiculous and pessimistic, and he went further into his shell. Our relationship was tense, and I felt like it could all fall apart at any moment.

It was a cold morning in the beginning of December 1992 when Jack finally broke down and told me the truth about everything. We were two weeks away from moving into our long awaited dream home, and three weeks away from the birth of our second child. He confessed that in his absence Rusty had double crossed him, robbed him blind, sabotaged his business, and was forming a partnership that would put Jack under. We would have to declare bankruptcy, and we would have to give up the house. I was numb. I didn't cry, I didn't yell, I just accepted it. I was disappointed that everything I had worked so hard for would now be in vain, but I supported my husband, and tried to be strong for his sake. It always kind of bothered me that I never saw the inside of the house completed, but it took me years to acknowledge the pain caused by having that rug pulled out from underneath me. We truly had been living a lie.

Christmas was solemn that year. I think Jack slept through it. I used to hold Alexis on my lap and hug her when I was sad. She emanated an energy that

97

could make me feel whole again in an instant. It was as if I could squeeze the love out of her and let it flow into me. She saved me from going mad, and I was able to be stoic for her sake. I couldn't tell my parents what was going on because they were already starting to voice their concerns, and I didn't want them to hate my husband.

Chapter 13

A shadow of myself

Jack managed to drag himself out of bed to take me to the hospital on December 28, 1992 to give birth to our second daughter, Ashley. This time more of my family had come to support me, sensing that it was a rough patch for us, and that we would need help with Alexis. As much discomfort as I was feeling from being pregnant, I was not ready for more responsibility. I couldn't imagine having more diapers to change, more midnight feedings, or more needy cries to attend to. I was overwhelmed.

Again, I begged Dr. Schaeffer to tie my tubes, but once more he refused. He reminded me how young I was, and pointed out how old Jack was, and insisted that some day I would want to have more children with my next husband. I didn't fight with him, though, because I could finally see the wisdom of his words, and I was not feeling confident that my marriage would last.

Since we didn't have insurance anymore, my hospital stay was very brief. No sooner had they stitched me up then they shipped me home. My mother stayed and cared for me for about a week, until I was back on my feet. I resented having to share my time with this new child. I was angry that the new baby screamed and cried and could not be consoled. She was not warm and cuddly, she was a manifestation of my unhappiness, and it was quite apparent. The only one she accepted solace from was Jack, and he was not in any frame of mind to give a shit. This was quite a different experience from a year before. Our apartment was filled with dark energy, depression, and hopelessness. Alexis remained my only comfort, and I held her tightly whenever possible.

It amazed me that Jack could sleep through the night when Ashley was screaming. He had been so helpful with Alexis, but his pride was now hurt, and he escaped the despair by sleeping. His diabetes was also causing problems, but he refused to take his medicine even tough he had a full bottle of it sitting on the counter. We could barely pay the rent, but he couldn't keep a job for more than a week. He worked at 7-11 for a while, and then a gas station down the street, but he always came up with some example of how the establishment was persecuting him, or some reason that his job was beneath him. We had no money for diapers, but he still managed to scrape up enough for three packs of cigarettes a day. My family was clueless, or they would have helped, but I knew that their way of helping would be to offer me a place at home, and I was not willing to give up hope for my marriage yet. I knew they wouldn't forgive Jack for how he was neglecting me, so I remained silent and desperate for a light at the end of this tunnel. I was embarrassed by how my life was spiraling downward, and I didn't want anyone to know how close I was to blowing my brains out. Had I not thought that Alexis would be scarred by the absence of her natural mother, or had I not been so curious and determined to see how she would grow up, and what she would become in life, I would most definitely have ended it all. My love for Alexis was greater than the pain, so I managed to endure it, even if it was one slow, miserable, torturous day at a time.

One night when Ashley was less than two weeks old, she was having one of her temper tantrums. I hadn't slept or eaten in days, and I was shaking from the stress and fatigue. As she wailed louder and louder, something in me snapped, and I took the pillow from behind my back and held it over her tiny little face. I fantasized about holding it there until she shut up. I planned to grab Alexis and run far, far away, never returning to this fucking hell. Luckily, the voice in my head returned and coaxed me into lifting the pillow. Ashley was no worse for the wear, and I held her close, kissed her innocent little head, and begged her forgiveness, and that of the Lord. It was not that I didn't love her...far from it, really. I felt like she hated me and that I had failed her by bringing her into this shitty situation. I didn't want her to have to experience this hopeless life with such worthless parents. It was in that instant I knew that it was up to me to pull my family out of the gutter. I knew that Jack was no longer capable of caring for us, and that I needed to take action. My girls deserved to be healthy, happy, and provided for. I could be strong for them, even if I couldn't be strong for myself.

The next morning as I sympathetically watched reports of how a man in France, Jean Claude Romand, killed his family and tried to burn himself inside his home, I called the Department of Welfare and attempted to get some assistance. At first they were eager to help me, but when I started answering their questions the response lost enthusiasm. First, they asked me what my race was. Caucasian was the wrong answer. Next they asked me if I was married. Yes was the wrong answer to that. The woman on the other end of the line begged me to say that I thought we would be splitting up, but I could not. I wanted to help Jack too. She asked if my husband was in jail, and I could hear the disappointment in her voice when I told her that he was not, nor did I think he would be any time soon. I explained that we were a hard working married couple who had fallen upon difficult times, and that we just needed a hand getting back on the right track, but that is apparently not the demographic that welfare intends to serve. It was at that precise moment when I decided to become a Republican.

Once I realized that Democrat social programs were not going to be the key, I started interviewing for jobs. I went on nearly a dozen interviews, and, for the first time in my life, no one would hire me. I had a great resume for my age, having been employed since I was 9, and plenty of skills, but when they heard that I had a one year old and an infant at home they felt that I would be unreliable. Everyone I talked to told me I was crazy. They urged me to kick my husband in the ass and for me to spend the necessary time with my babies. Several offered to give HIM a job, but refused to take me away from my kids no matter how badly we needed the money. I explained that the bill collectors called so often I was on a first name, friendly basis with them. I was stressed beyond belief, and we really needed something good to happen for us in a hurry. Nothing worked though, and no one would give me a job.

I was at the end of my rope. We all needed a change of scenery and a little fresh air, so we packed up the minivan and headed down to Georgia to see Jack's mother. She had not yet met Ashley, and they were not healthy enough to travel, so it seemed like a great opportunity. I hoped that the long stretches of open road would provide me with some clarity.

It ended up being a nice visit and it gave me an opportunity to feel Jack out about being a stay at home dad. He was all for it, and it renewed his hope that he could contribute to our well being, even if it wasn't monetary support, which he was no longer confident he could provide. It must have been a difficult time for him, too. He was a broken down 44 year old man with a 21 year old wife and two tiny children, and no prospects for gainful employment. His business had gone down the tubes and he failed to even hold a minimum wage job at a convenience store. Worst of all, he couldn't begin to fuck his young wife. I'm sure he felt pretty morose and useless. I tried to comfort him and make him believe that we'd be alright. At the same time I was attempting to convince myself.

As Jack drove, I flipped through a local special interest paper, Style Weekly. There I saw an ad for a female hostess that caught my attention. It sounded like good hours, great money, and something I could really excel at, entertaining business men. I called the minute we got home. Of course, the first thing I wanted to make sure of was that this was not prostitution. The man on the other end of the line assured me that there was no sex involved, and that it was purely above board. These were simply men who needed a little bit of company, maybe someone to join them for dinner or intellectual conversation. "Perfect," I thought. I knew I'd be great at that. Besides, it would get me out of the house, and I could spend my time discussing something besides "Barney" or "Rugrats." I looked in the phone book and, sure enough, they had a full page color ad. They had to be legitimate if they were in the Yellow Pages, I thought. I gladly, blindly, and naively accepted the job with Aaadrien's Escort Service.

Chapter 14

She makes house calls

I was instructed to get a pager so that the agency could contact me 24 hours a day. Within minutes of having it activated I was beeped for an assignment. I called into the office and was given the phone number of a gentleman who required my company. Just to be sure, I went back over the facts with my new boss, Tony. I wanted to be certain that no sex was involved, and that this was strictly a professional service. In his deep, gritty, smoker's voice he reassured me, "Just do what you are comfortable with." That was good enough for me. Even though I'd never met Tony, he seemed confident and supportive, and I figured he knew what he was talking about. It struck me as odd when he advised me that his name would change periodically, that we would never meet face to face, and that I would never be told where he was located, but I suspended my better judgment for the sake of having a job.

Nervous and eager all at the same time, I dialed the number that Tony supplied. The guy who answered the phone seemed to be as unfamiliar with the process as I was, but we stumbled through the formalities and before long he had given me directions, and I was in my car on the way to his house. I had no idea what to expect when I knocked on the door of the small ranch home in Lakeside, a very blue collar section of town. I wondered how someone who lived here would have $400 to blow on something like this.

A meek but towering guy with stringy long brown hair wearing jeans and a Def Leopard shirt answered the door. He appeared to be in his late 30's. I shook his hand and introduced myself, and he told me that his name was Chris. It was the middle of the day, but we sat in his living room with the shades drawn, and made idle conversation. I was to collect my fee upfront, and to call the office to let them know I had received the payment. They also wanted to monitor the time so that I didn't spend more than the allotted hour without being compensated. Chris and I both looked at our watches, not sure quite what to do. I could tell that he wanted to ask me something, but was too shy to do it. Finally he worked up the courage to bring up the topic of sex. I bluntly told him that I had no intention of fucking him, that I was there for companionship only, and that he had 47 minutes left to discuss whatever else might be on his mind. I could tell he was bummed, and he apologized for offending me, explaining that he thought he had ordered a hooker. I told him that I'd just had a baby 3 weeks prior, and that I had a huge gaping surgical wound that would bust open if I did anything of the sort. I was still not cleared by the doctor to have sex with my own husband, let alone some stranger. He took it very well considering the amount of money that he had forked out for this mistake. I kind of felt bad for him, so when he asked if I'd be willing to massage his back I happily agreed. We did that for a while, and then he wanted to play me a song on his guitar. He was a sweet kid, and I felt blessed to have gotten him as my first appointment. I realized that I was in a very compromising position being in his home alone with him, and that he could have taken advantage of that if it had been his nature.

I called the office once more to let them know that I was leaving, and gave Chris a big hug goodbye. He seemed satisfied, and said that he would ask for me again. I had to drop $150 into a FedEx envelope that the escort service had provided, and mail it off to California as their split of the profits. I was more than happy to do that, though, because I now had $250 in my hand, and I hadn't been away from my babies very long. It would have taken me a week as a waitress to achieve the same results, and I just wasn't prepared to commit that time away from my young daughters.

When I got back home Jack seemed very aloof. He didn't want to hear details about what had happened; he just wanted to see the cash. We piled the girls in the minivan and immediately went grocery shopping. It felt amazing to put whatever I desired or needed into the cart. We had been running low on diapers, and could barely afford to buy Ashley's baby formula. I was proud that I could now provide for my family, and hope began to trickle back into my consciousness. I was grateful and empowered by this whole experience. The Lord had certainly opened a door that would make life smoother from here on out.

My pager began to vibrate while we were in the checkout line. I handed Jack the cash and went outside to use the pay phone, eager to accept my next assignment. This time I would visit a guy in a hotel room at the Embassy Suites. He was here on business from New Jersey and didn't know a soul in Richmond, so he was lonely. I was to arrive at 10 PM. That was great since it gave me time to have dinner with the kids, give them their baths, and make sure they were in bed before I left.

I sensed a knowing glare from the night attendant as the double doors opened, spitting me out into the palm tree filled atrium of the hotel. I made my way to the elevator, and it carried me to the 7th floor, where my next adventure was waiting.

The door to room 715 was propped open for me, so I entered without knocking. The man sitting patiently inside reading a newspaper caught me off guard because he was so attractive, not at all what I expected. Probably in his early 50's, Roger was a sophisticated, scholarly gentleman with a neatly trimmed beard, wearing an elegant three piece suit. There was a certain ease about him as he rose to greet me, and I was uncharacteristically comfortable. We had an electric, intellectual chemistry that was immediately apparent. I was not feeling great about my physical body, having gained at least 30 pounds from my two pregnancies, so this spark between us came as a surprise. At first glance I was afraid that I might not be his idea of a suitable cohort, but his actions were telling me otherwise. He held my hand, put his arm around me, and kissed my neck as we discussed payment options. He chose to pay by credit card, and did not hesitate to add a $50 tip. I called my boss and our hour began.

As I hung up the phone I turned around to find Roger completely naked on the bed in the next room. Oh, shit…this one was not going to take no for an answer quite as easily. I was so horny that part of me wanted to just fuck the crap out of him, but my C-section scar was still not healed and I was in a tight girdle to keep everything together. His cock was long and stiff, and his hairy chest begged me to nuzzle into it and ravage this man. I wanted to give back the money and pretend that we had met far more innocently, but that was unrealistic. I was determined not to be a prostitute, either, and this guy was not going to break my moral stance. As strange as it may seem, I have always been somewhat of a rule follower. I was just trying to earn a living. I didn't want to break any laws, just make an honest, if not conventional paycheck.

My mind began racing, seeking a solution to this growing dilemma. How was I going to make this work for everyone without compromising who I was? By the grace of God it came to me immediately. I sat on the side of the bed and began engaging Roger in an erotic conversation. He was stroking himself, but I didn't see any harm in that as long as I didn't touch him. Skillfully guiding the dialogue, I asked him what his deepest, darkest fantasies were. He gladly told me about wanting to be with two women at once, and how he enjoyed being tied up. I rubbed my nipples through my shirt, and pretended like I was getting really worked up with anticipation. I told him that I would love to help him live out those fantasies next time we got together. He squirted some lube into his palm and asked me what my fantasies were. I feigned shyness to add to the illusion and to manipulate him into feeling a sense of urgency. He became eager to unlock the supposed depths of my perversion, and after I orchestrated him to persuade me more adamantly, I "reluctantly" gave in.

"It's really embarrassing," I confessed in a soft voice, "but I've always wanted to hide in the closet and watch a guy jerk off without him knowing that I was there."

"Let's do it!" Roger urged, as if it was now his fantasy too. He was right where I wanted him, and my plan was almost too good. I couldn't believe that such a brilliant man had so easily fallen into my trap.

I walked slowly and sensuously to the closet opposite the bed, and slipped inside, leaving the door slightly ajar. Although the view was obstructed, I could hear the slurping sounds of his hand vigorously jerking his rock solid member. I was wet as hell, and wanted nothing more than to go help him, but knew it was inappropriate. Within a minute or two I heard him gasp loudly, pant a bit, and then let out a sigh of relief. Mission accomplished. He got up to grab a towel from the bathroom and I snuck out the door, ran down the emergency stairs, hopped in my car and drove away. I was delighted to have outwitted my circumstance.

On the way home I was forced to confront the fact that I had been mislead. No man in his right mind was paying that much money to chat with a woman. It was really stupid for me to have believed it, even in my desperation. Still, I would try my new routine out on the next guy and see how it worked. At the rate I was going we would be back on our feet in no time, and with a cushion in the bank. That would make it easier to have a normal job and still feel like we could make ends meet.

True to form, Jack didn't inquire how my night had gone. He sat on the couch drinking iced tea, smoking his cigarettes, and watching an old John Wayne movie on television. He acted like I'd just returned from a book club meeting or something, not concerned a bit.

It was nearly 2 AM when the pager went off again. This time I was summoned to the Comfort Inn on Jefferson Davis Highway. It was a long drive, and not a particularly safe place for a woman to be at this hour, but I had the money on my mind, so I went. Again, my client was a middle aged, decent looking guy, well mannered, but lonely. He fed into my plan, and I was only with him for about thirty minutes with absolutely no physical contact. He did it all himself! This was almost too good to be true, and I feared that this could not go on indefinitely. I had made $800 on my first day without doing anything I couldn't live with.

Day two is one that I'll never forget. It was a real turning point in my life. Around 11 PM I was assigned to the Hilton to visit a very amiable, handsome man who gave me his business card and told me his name was Theodore Vincent, and that he was a local veterinarian. He was trite and methodical once we were alone in his room. He offered me the cash and sat on the bed with his head in his hands.

"You've got to get out of this line of work," he warned me. "It's not safe, and you're going to get killed. I don't want anything from you, and you can leave as soon as you listen to my story. I booked this appointment so I could tell you to quit your job. My girlfriend was working for this escort service, but now she is in the hospital in critical condition, and we don't expect her to live. She went out on a call where a man brutally raped her, savagely beat her, busted in her skull, and left her for dead. It was a miracle that she survived at all, but we don't think she's going to pull through. The guy is still on the loose, and I don't want this to happen to any more women, so I'm begging you to stop."

Wow…It was suddenly very clear to me that I was playing Russian roulette with my life. I was so touched by the fact that this man was willing to shell out $400 to warn me of this danger that I promised him I would quit immediately, in spite of my need for the money. I knew that what he was saying was true, and I didn't take the information lightly. I knew in my heart that this was not a random event. I understood that this man had been sent by God to protect me. I wept as I drove home, feeling like I had been spared great tragedy by having been given this information.

This time Jack paid attention as I walked through the door, having just left home 30 minutes prior. My face was a mess, and he asked what was wrong. I recounted the story of what had happened to the best of my ability through the tears and hysteria. Jack seemed untouched by the revelation.

"Oh, that's hogwash," he exclaimed. "That guy was just trying to scare you!"

"Well, he succeeded. I can't do it anymore. It's just not worth taking the risk. How are you going to raise two infants if I get murdered?" I asked him. "It just doesn't feel right anymore. It's not what they told me it would be, these guys expect sex, and I can't ignore that this was all a very bad decision. I got lucky for a while. I made us some money, and that's great, but I'm finished."

"I can't believe how fucking selfish you are to even think about quitting now," Jack said with rage in his eyes. "You WILL keep doing it...end of discussion. Now, wipe yourself up. You're a mess."

I was a mess, because it was in that instant that I knew my marriage was over. How could this man who was supposed to love and protect me... the father of my children...pimp me out like this for the sake of his own laziness and inadequacy? I was mortally wounded by Jack's reaction. I stood staring at my pathetic, puffy, wet face in the bathroom mirror, trying to sort through my emotions. Should I just take the kids and leave him now? Could he ever repair the damage he had done to me tonight? Would I ever feel safe with this man again knowing how little he values me? How could my life at 21 years old be so fucked up and senseless? A million questions and judgments raced through my throbbing head. I felt alone and despondent and began withdrawing into myself when my pager went off in the next room, snapping me back to clear conscience. Jack appeared in the doorway, holding the pager, shaking it at me like it was our lifeline. It was almost 3 AM, and here I was getting another call. "I just can't do it, Jack...not tonight...not right now," I sobbed.

"You can and you will! Now, go make the phone call and see where they're sending you," Jack ordered without shame or regret.

I did as I was told, although life would never be the same for us now that this line had been drawn in the sand. I was fully aware now of where I stood in my marriage. I took off my wedding ring and went on the appointment. When I came home Jack was asleep on the couch. I threw the money at him, waking him from some pleasant dream, and locked myself in the bedroom. I needed to be alone with my pain. I needed time to think. I wanted so desperately to call my mother, but I knew that she'd be disgusted and hurt by this whole situation. I didn't want the rest of my family to know, either. I couldn't just dump this on my mom and expect that she wouldn't need someone to talk to, and that person would probably be my grandmother, who, in turn, would need to talk to someone else… and on and on until everyone knew my business. I had never been particularly good about keeping secrets, but I felt like this was the perfect opportunity to practice.

Chapter 15

An angel has many faces

I could no longer fool myself into believing that what I was doing was safe or rational. Every time my pager went off I jumped. I wondered whether the next guy would be the one who would murder me, or what would happen if I were left beaten in some dirty motel room. A different survival instinct had kicked in. For a time my main concern had been putting food on the table, but now it was all about staying alive for my babies. Ignorance truly was bliss, but I didn't have that fog to protect me anymore. I decided to be more alert, and to just get the hell out of any situation that might feel uncomfortable. I constantly prayed for my protection, and tried to have faith that I was surrounded by celestial security. The past weeks had been a roller coaster ride of mixed blessings, moral challenges, and deep inner struggle.

Without giving him details, I hinted to my father on the phone that Jack and I were having some issues. His love and respect was not quite as important to me as that of the rest of my family, so I figured that he was a good place to start. Even if the cat got out of the bag, I didn't really care what he thought. I almost wanted him to know what a nightmare my life had become. It was nice to be able to let some of my worries loose, and things didn't appear quite as bad once I had a chance to verbalize what I was feeling. Everything had been so internalized to this point that it was eating me up inside. Maybe I *was* just being selfish?

My father reminded me how badly it affected us children when he and my mom split up. He asked me if that was really what I wanted for my kids. Of course it wasn't. I needed to try harder so that they would grow up in a stable home with both of their parents. I couldn't let them suffer just to make my life easier. I thought about Grandma Christie. Her husband had been mean and abusive, but she had stayed, making a life for herself separate from his. I could do that too. I would find my own happiness wherever it presented itself.

I resolved to keep plugging away at my marriage, and to try to do my job more joyfully. Had my dad known exactly what I was talking about, his advice would have been quite different, I am sure. Still, his encouragement was what I needed to be able to stay in my current situation, and I had nowhere else to go.

My pager was vibrating on the counter, but it didn't bother me quite as much as it had before. I acknowledged that this was my lot in life for the moment, and I just had to suck it up and be strong.

I accepted an appointment for 10 PM, took a shower, and began getting dressed. My incision was painful, but gradually healing. It stung as I squirmed to get into the thick girdle I had to wear under my miniskirt. Even with it on I still didn't look very good. "Man," I thought, "If these guys only knew who they were getting... a fat housewife with two babies and a worthless husband...they would hang up that phone and order a pizza instead." I could not feel lower about myself.

Before I walked out the door I always went in the girls' room to kiss them goodbye and make sure they were okay. Tonight as I watched them sleep peacefully in their cribs, tears filled my eyes. All I could think about was the fact that there was a possibility that I would never see them again. Instead of stepping out for an hour or two, I might be saying farewell forever. It killed me. It wounded my spirit to have to leave them. I wasn't afraid of death; I was just worried about who would take care of them if I was gone. Would they even remember me? What would they be told? I wiped the tears on my sleeve and slipped out, not waking them.

The crisp, cold night air helped breathe life back into me. It was good to be out of the apartment, and I cherished the alone time walking through the parking lot to the car. For a moment I almost forgot what I was doing and where I was going. I was at peace with my circumstance, and gave thanks to the Lord for filling me with the strength to keep going.

I played loud music and sang at the top of my lungs as I drove to the Super 8. I released all of the negative thoughts in my head, and embraced the moment. Maybe this would be another good one.

The parking spot was open in front of room 112, so I took it, appreciating the serendipity, and taking it as a good sign. After a quick check in the mirror to make sure there was nothing stuck in my teeth, I got out of the car and knocked on the door. It seemed like an eternity before Paul answered my incessant tapping. I wondered if he had changed his mind, but then the knob turned. He was shaking with fear, short, slightly overweight, and balding a bit on the top of his head. I think he was actually relieved to see that I was pretty average looking, not some hot vamp that would pull out the whips and chains.

One of the first things I noticed about him was his wedding band. It was a bit dented, and looked like the shine had been gone from it for a number of years. As he handed me the money I nodded my head as if pointing to his finger and asked him how long he had been married.

"16 years next month," he sighed. "I love her more than anything in the world." Peter now had me very confused.

"Okay…wait a minute…you've got to explain," I begged him, completely fascinated by the notion of a happily married man hiring an escort. "Why am I here?"

"Beth and I have been together since we were 15. We dated for 5 years, and we've been married almost 16. I can't imagine living without her. She is perfect in every way, and we have 4 incredible children. I don't have a single complaint about her. We have a wonderful, exciting sex life. Everything is like a dream, but I have one nagging regret. We are both devout Catholics, and were virgins when we got married. She is the only woman I have ever been with, and I'm afraid that I'll die having only made

118

love to one woman. I would feel more complete as a man if you would be willing to help me change that tonight. I think I'd be a better husband if I could stop thinking about everything I missed out on."

Paul's intense love and devotion for his wife really touched my heart, and I felt desperation to help him, but not in the way he had anticipated. We sat at the small round table in the corner of his room facing each other. I reached out to hold both of his hands so that he could focus on what I needed to tell him. Our eyes locked, and I spoke slowly and clearly so that the words might sink in and really resonate with him.

"You have been given a precious gift that most people search their entire lives for. You have found your perfect match. She loves you, has given you a wonderful family, and has devoted her life to making you happy. Not many people can say that they are still in love after so many years. What you have is so very rare and valuable. I have been with many men in my life, but only because I was searching for the one who could make me feel the way Beth makes you feel every day. It is far more beautiful to know that you two are pure in your love. You give each other something that you have never offered anyone else, and that is to be celebrated, not lamented. You two have a one in a million situation. Once you ruin that, it's over, it can never be repaired. You will have taken everything that is sacred for you and your wife and squandered it on something meaningless that you won't even be able to enjoy. You won't be able to have me without thinking about her the entire time. Then, your guilt will overcome you, and you won't be able to live with yourself. Not to mention the fact that by having sex with another woman you can expose Beth to diseases and infections that could permanently harm her. Is that what you want? You have paid your $400, and if you still desire the experience of fucking another woman, I am here for you," I said to him, as if some ancient being had channeled the message through my body.

Paul paused and thought for several minutes, never realizing that my offer was not genuine. I couldn't imagine being the one to tarnish something so beautiful and sweet, but I felt like he needed to feel like it was a possibility and make his own decision. A big part of his angst was that he had never had the opportunity, so I surmised that now that the opportunity was presenting itself, he would feel validated in his choice to pass it up, and that may be enough to ease his mind.

Tears welled in Paul's eyes. He grabbed me and hugged me. "You are an angel," he beamed. "You have prevented me from making the biggest mistake of my life. How can I ever thank you enough?"

"You can thank me by leaving here right now, going home to your beautiful wife, and never worrying about such foolishness again. Value what you have, and don't let anyone tell you that what they can offer may be better, because it's not," I urged him. "Meeting you tonight has been a blessing to me. Now I know that the love I search for really exists. It's not just a fairy tale. You have inspired me to reach higher, and…I must thank *you* for that."

He packed up his things and we left the motel together, two souls encountering one another for a brief moment, but exchanging the lessons of a lifetime. I walked on air; feeling in perfect alignment with my life's calling, knowing that I had just been a part of something monumental. Deep inside there was a sadness, though, because I couldn't share what had just happened with anyone else. God's divine love had shone through me tonight, and it was part of the secret I needed to keep.

For the first time in a while, I slept soundly, and woke up early the next morning to play with Alexis and Ashley. We rolled around on the floor together, and enjoyed a few moments of silliness. It was only 9 AM when my pager started going off. That was unusual, but it might mean the start to a profitable day. I was still flying high from the night before, and couldn't wait to see what was around the next corner. My fear had momentarily diminished.

Noon saw me pulling into the driveway of a Mr. Frank Ellis on Monument Ave. It was a huge brick house on a much esteemed block of the most prestigious street in Richmond. This is where the old money was. "Interesting," I thought, making a snap judgment about whom and what I might find inside, when really I had no idea.

As I approached the home I saw the silhouette of a person in an upstairs window. Someone was peeking through the curtains watching me meander along the cobblestone walkway. Suddenly, the front door opened, and an elderly man in a sweater vest and bowtie came out to greet me. It took me off guard because it seemed too quick for him to have been able to come all the way down the stairs. I snuck a peek back at the window, and realized that it was someone else spying on me. "I'm sorry," I said apologetically, thinking I had the wrong address, "I'm looking for a Mr. Ellis."

"Oh, yes, you're in the wrong place then, dear. Mr. Ellis is my father, and he's been dead for many years. I'm Frank. Hearing someone refer to me as Mr. Ellis makes me feel old, and I'm having no part in that."

"Sorry, Frank...I didn't mean to imply anything. I'm Vicki," I said as he ushered me in the door. His foyer was as big as my apartment, and full of gorgeous antiques and Oriental rugs. Frank handed me an envelope, and I tucked it in my purse, thanking him.

"This is all my wife's idea," he began matter-of-factly. "She feels guilty that she hasn't been able to pleasure me in a very long time, and she insisted that I find someone to take care of me once in a while. I'm a bit old for the dating scene, so I thought I'd try this route."

"Is that who I saw in the window upstairs?" I questioned him.

"Yes, she is very impatient, but she wants to make sure it's the right kind of girl. I think she's crazy, but I've always tried to make her happy. Really, I don't want any part of this whole thing. She's been sick with cancer for the past ten years, and I think it's finally getting the best of her. I'll feel lucky if she makes it to summer. You're a beautiful woman. I think she'd be pleased with you."

I blushed at the compliment, not actually believing that I was very pretty anymore, but thankful for the kind words all the same. "Are you scared of losing her?" I blurted out, afraid that maybe I should

122

have censored myself, but intrinsically knowing that this man probably needed to talk about what he was feeling.

"Terrified, but she's in so much pain. I hate to see her that way." Tears started rolling down Frank's face, and he pulled a white handkerchief from his pocket to wipe away his despair. His youthful demeanor disappeared as he slumped into a wingback chair near his fireplace. I sat at his feet, hugging his frail legs, and resting my head on his lap. I could feel him shaking, so I held him tightly for several minutes until he was able to compose himself.

"I can only imagine what you're going through. Death is a very difficult process, and it seems like you've been watching it for a long time." I offered, trying to be as tender and compassionate as I knew how. "Maybe you can try to focus on the good years you've had. Enjoy her while she's still here."

"That's what I want," Frank gleamed, surprised that I would be so astute. "Emily is so concerned about what will become of me when she's gone she has pulled away already so it will be easier when it happens. She wants me to replace her now so she can go without guilt. I want to hold her and comfort her, but she does all she can to keep me at a distance."

"Can we go up so that I can meet her?"

"Yes, she would like that," he beamed, regaining his energy.

Frank led me up the wide center staircase, past the balcony, and down a few doors to a lovely room with flowered wallpaper and a double canopy bed. I surmised that this may have been their daughter's room at one point, and that Emily might have chosen it during her illness for the sunlight that poured through the numerous windows. She was now neatly tucked beneath a fluffy down comforter with her eyes closed. It was obvious that she had been a stunning woman in her day, with elegant bone structure and delicately pleasing features. Her hair was flowing and silver, framing her face on the pillow. Frank touched her on the arm and she woke with a slight start. She knew who I was and why I was there, and she tried to lift herself up to greet me. Apparently her time at the window had worn her out, and it was all she could do to raise her arm to shake my hand. I sat in a small café chair next to her bed and spoke softly to her as Frank hovered behind me, unsure of what I might say.

"You are very kind to be so concerned for your husband. It's obvious that you love each other immensely," I said as I gently held her fragile hand. "Sex with strangers will not make Frank's pain any easier. What he needs right now is you."

Emily smiled and her eyes brightened momentarily. Without saying a word, perhaps because she was unable, she pulled the blanket to one side, and gingerly made room next to her. Frank kicked off his shoes and carefully lay beside her, pulling the comforter over both of them, and putting his arm around his wife. Not a sound was uttered by any of us. I kissed them each on the forehead and showed myself to the door.

I cried bittersweet tears as I pulled away from the house. I was happy to have been a catalyst for healthy change, but grieved for the realization that I would probably never know a love that strong for myself. It also seemed bizarre that my days as a hooker were filled with therapy instead of sex. I was thankful for that, but I could no longer be victimized by my husband's insistence that I do this job. He would have to find work, and I needed to relearn how to stand up for what I knew to be right. I used to be so confident and self assured, but I had let that part of my personality slide into the background. I had lost myself in the endless shuffle. No one would even have recognized me as the same girl I was 2 years ago. I wasn't a person at all anymore.

Jack and the children were at the store when I got home. Apparently I had forgotten my pager, because it was sitting on the counter with a note underneath it. It said Hyatt, East Main, 8 PM, Room C25, Tim Fitz. "This is the last one," I promised myself.

I stretched out on the couch and turned on the television. Geraldo was doing a show about Skinheads and all of the chaos and violence they were causing around the country. I couldn't believe that white supremacists even existed in this day and age, but apparently they did, and they were viciously angry. He was showing members of the Aryan Nation. They were really good looking young guys. I was shocked. This wasn't the kind of stuff I wanted to fill my head with, though, so I hit the off button and took a nap instead.

Chapter 16

Tim Fitz

I left early for my appointment at the Hyatt because the rain was pouring down in sheets, and I could barely see the road in front of me. I knew I had to proceed slowly, and I didn't want to be in a rush. I drove the minivan so that my visibility would be slightly better, but nothing really helped. I was angry to be out on such a nasty evening, and resolved that no matter what, this would be my last client ever. Something just didn't feel right.

It was no easy task to find C25, so I got the bellman to give me directions. I couldn't help but notice that he winced when I told him which room I wanted, and I began to get paranoid. The C building was quite a walk from the more populated part of the hotel. I didn't even know it existed until now. The lobby had been bustling with guests, but this hallway seemed dark, narrow, and deserted. The other corridors had been lined with room service carts and signs of life, but this one was barren. Many of the light bulbs in the ceiling fixtures were burned out. It was as if I were in the dungeon.

I usually felt a certain level of comfort when I was at a nice hotel. I thought that in the worst case scenario if I screamed someone would hear me and try to find out what was going on. Every hair on my body was standing up, and I nearly turned around and said "screw it," but I knew Jack would be pissed and it would ignite a huge argument. I just wasn't up for that tonight, so I knocked on the door, said a quick prayer for protection, and held my breath.

A sense of foreboding overwhelmed me as Tim Fitz opened the door. He wasn't what I had grown accustomed to. He was young, great looking, and arrogant. He did not fit the profile of my previous clients, and alarms started going off in my head. He was too young, too blonde, and not the least bit nervous. I began to sweat, and my breathing was labored. I surveyed the room carefully, looking for any signs of danger. My blood ran cold as I noticed a book on the dresser with a swastika on it. It was some Nazi paraphernalia. There was another one on the nightstand along with a drink and a cigarette, still burning. "You smoke?" I asked him.

"No, do you?" he replied.

I gulped and tried to remain calm, not sure what all of this meant. I poked my head in the bathroom to make sure we were alone. He put the money on the table and I took it and placed it in my purse. His phone was dead when I tried to call Tony to check in. I was gripped by fear. There was no small talk, no getting to know each other, no politeness; he just started telling me what he expected me to do. I told him that I was uncomfortable with his requests since that was not how I operated. I offered to return his money and contact one of the other girls, but that did not satisfy him. He started ripping off his clothes and then began tugging at mine. When I resisted him he grabbed my wrists and told me that we were playing by his rules now. I started to cry, and explained to him that I'd just had a baby and was unable to have sex with him. He pulled my shirt over my head, against my will, and tore my bra. "I'm not comfortable with this!" I yelled, hoping to attract some attention, but he seized my arm, cupped my mouth, and told me to shut the fuck up. I kept repeating the same words over and over to him in a softer, more vulnerable voice. "I'm just not comfortable. This is not what I do. I'm just not comfortable."

By now I was in full terror mode. I believed that at minimum I would be raped, and resigned myself to that fact. I knew I could endure it; I just needed to get out alive. I would still try to talk my way around it, but I would be more cooperative so that he would not be forced to use his strength. I said another silent prayer and tried once again to engage him in conversation. He seemed to relax a bit, and I was encouraged until he took off his pants. He was naked except for his boxers and some white socks, and he began touching me inappropriately. He pulled down my skirt, leaving me nude, with the exception of my girdle, which he was trying to pry off. "I have a surgical wound. You can't take it off. My stitches will burst." I begged him to show some mercy.

"I'll make you a deal," he said slyly as he got on the bed, propping his back against the pillows and crossing his legs at the ankles. "All I need you to do is to get up here on the bed with me and bend over on your knees like you would if you were giving me head. Then I'll let you leave."

The request seemed bizarre, as if he had an agenda, but I couldn't figure out where he was going with it, and I thought it might be my ticket to freedom, so I followed his instructions. As soon as I was in position he said, "Man, I wish my friend Woody could see me now," and 6 men burst through the door from the adjoining room with guns. My heart literally stopped. I thought they were his buddies, and that I was about to be gang raped and probably murdered. I was literally paralyzed. Tim jumped off the bed and put his clothes back on, and one of the guys started reciting something. Now I was totally confused. It took me a few moments, and then I became aware that these guys were cops, and one was reading me my Miranda rights. I wasn't going to be gang banged, I was being arrested.

One of the guys tossed me my clothes as another rifled through my purse. He reported to the others that I didn't have any drugs or weapons. He sounded surprised. I could tell that they were caught a bit off guard by the fact that I was not the kind of person they anticipated. By now I was thanking them for arresting me. I explained that this was not something I wanted to do, and that now my husband would have no choice but to listen. The gentleman processing me said that if I cooperated this would be a breeze; that it was not me they were after, they wanted to get to the head of the snake. I told him everything I knew about the organization, but I sensed that they thought I was holding back. He said that since I didn't have any prior convictions I shouldn't bother to get a lawyer. He said that everything was on tape, and that I would have access to the recording as my defense. He seized my pager, all of the contents of my purse except my driver's license, and then he asked what kind of car I was driving. I told him it was a minivan we had just purchased a few months ago. Apparently, had I driven the Mustang, which I had some equity in; they would have confiscated and sold that as punishment as well. Thank goodness it had been raining, or I would not have had a car to drive home. Someone upstairs had really been watching out for me.

When they were done with me they released me on one condition: I was not to tell my boss that I had been arrested under any circumstance. I thanked them and fumbled my way out of the hotel. I couldn't help but recognize the irony in the fact that being humiliated and arrested was actually an improvement over my prior situation. Even if Jack wouldn't listen to me, he would have to listen to the cops, and my career as an escort would be over. Really, my troubles were just starting, but, for the moment I felt like a huge weight had been lifted off my shoulders. Unfortunately, I failed to hear the rapid whistling of the boulder plummeting out of the sky, directed toward my head.

Chapter 17

Hell and brim fire

My ride home was full of gratitude and appreciation. Even though there had been some trying moments, I had not been raped or beaten, and I was on the way back to my babies. It had stopped raining, and I had a sense that all of the stars in the sky were there just for me. When I pulled into the parking lot I saw Jack out in the breezeway, sitting on the stairs smoking. "It's over," I told him, hands raised and palms up, showing him that it was now out of my control. "I thought I was going to get gang raped, but instead I got arrested. I'm going to help the cops catch Tony, and this should all blow over, but I'm going to have to find a new job."

Jack had been watching the local news and had seen a story about a sting operation that was being conducted across the county, so he wasn't surprised. He gave me a hug and we went inside. I looked in on the girls and found them sleeping peacefully; once again, blissfully unaware of the disaster they had been born into. "It's all over, pumpkins. You've got your mommy back," I whispered in their ears as I kissed their warm foreheads.

I went to bed but couldn't sleep. I recounted the night's events over and over again realizing statistically how "lucky" I had been to have fallen into the trap. Had I just been given a different appointment I would have been forced to do this vile job indefinitely. We would certainly miss the money, but I was free again, and that meant more to me than the cash. It was inopportune that we hadn't saved anything over the past weeks, but somehow we'd get by.

When the sun began to rise I decided to get up and take a shower. A new day and a new life were beginning, and I wanted to get an early start. Besides, I hadn't been able to quiet my mind long enough to sleep anyway. I was in the middle of washing my hair, deep in thoughtful meditation, when the bathroom door opened. I freaked out. I began to panic. Terror surged through me as I pulled the curtain from the hooks and wrapped it around me. I felt stupid when I realized it was just my husband. Jack was confused by my reaction, and I can't blame him because I was too. I couldn't catch my breath, and began gasping for oxygen. When the door had opened unexpectedly it brought back my memories of the more troubling aspects of the night before. Maybe I had been more deeply affected than I realized. Even though I had managed to put on a good game face and see the positive in the situation to get myself through, the trauma was now almost unbearable. I made him shut the door as I sat on the floor sobbing. My hair was nearly dry by the time I regained my composure.

It was only 7 AM, but the phone was ringing. I answered it, and immediately recognized the deep, antsy voice on the other end of the line. "Tony?" I asked.

"No, it's Rick now," the voice explained. "Why didn't you call me last night at the Hyatt? Why haven't you returned my pages? I've been trying to reach you for 8 hours, and I'm not happy."

Shit! What was I going to tell him without blowing my promise to the cops? "I can't do this anymore. I'm sorry," I said tensely.

"Nice try, you little bitch!" he screamed back. "You must have been with that guy all fucking night. You owe me a goddamn thousand dollars, and it better get to me by tomorrow morning or you're fucking dead. You can't fuck with me like this. You have no clue who I am. This is not a game, this is a matter of life and death, you fucking whore."

He hung up before I could explain. I didn't know who to be more afraid of, Tony or the cops. My gut told me that Tony might be far more of a force to be reckoned with than the police. What could they do, throw me in jail? Obviously, Tony would have no problem whacking me and moving on. I wondered if that had been the case with the Vet's girlfriend. Maybe Tony was indirectly responsible for beating the crap out of her.

My life flashed before my eyes once again. My naïveté had gotten me tangled in a web of filth that I had no clue about. I always took people at their word, trusted everyone, but apparently I had misjudged this one. When I applied for this job I gave

"Tony" all of my information: real name, address, phone number, and even my social security number. Much worse, I told him about my kids. This guy knew everything about me and I knew nothing of him.

Detective Miller had given me his business card, so as soon as I got a grip on the urgency of my situation I called him. We arranged a meeting at Aunt Sarah's Restaurant down the street.

Ron Miller was a fat, stubby little guy in khakis and an Izod jacket. He wasn't much to look at, but he was my only hope. I hugged him like he was my long lost friend, and we entered the restaurant. I laughed to myself, realizing that the hostess had no idea what covert madness was going on right under her nose.

"What have you got for me?" he asked pointedly.

"What have I got for *you?*" I questioned in disbelief. "Since I can't tell my boss that I was arrested he thinks that I'm trying to fuck him over and he has threatened to kill my family. What have you got for me? I want to help you, I truly do, but you're going to have to offer me some sort of protection if you want me to play this game."

"No go. I can't do a thing. You got yourself into this and now you have to pay the piper. You're on your own. We may ask you to go on a few more appointments, but you're not to do anything until we tell you to. Just avoid his calls."

"Didn't you hear me?" I demanded. "He is going to kill me and my babies! He's demanding more money than I can come up with. He wants it tomorrow. What am I going to do? How are you guys going to explain the murdered white suburban family when he has his way with us?" I was exasperated. "If you can't guarantee our safety then there's nothing more I can do for you." I told him as I stood up and stormed out, nearly knocking the waitress off her feet as she approached the table to get our order. I shook my head in disbelief. How could the cops expect me to cooperate with them when I had a madman on my case? I felt powerless. I wanted with all of my heart to do the right thing, but I did expect that there would be some cloak of protection. Obviously, I was wrong.

"You're going to be very sorry!" the detective screamed at me as he followed me to the car.

"I'm afraid there's nothing more I can do for you if you can't guarantee my family's safety. I'm already in jeopardy." I sensed his anger and disgust as he processed my words. He looked at me like he thought I was hiding something, but really, I had told him everything I knew.

It seemed strange to me that he would think that I was holding out on him. Why wouldn't I want to help him? It wasn't as if I had any strong, meaningful ties to the escort service. It was just a job, and now that I knew that they really were doing something illegal, I actually wanted to assist.

It was only 4 PM, but I crawled into bed when I got home, weakened by the fear that had now gripped me. A cold chill rushed down my spine as the phone rang shortly thereafter. Jack answered it and brought me the cordless. It was Tony... or, Rick, as he was now calling himself.

"You fucking little dead bitch!" he greeted me. "The cops? You're having meetings with the cops now? You are so fucking dead, and Alexis and Ashley too. I'm going to let your husband live, though, so he can feel the pain of watching his entire family being snuffed."

I choked with horror, wondering how he knew what I had been doing just an hour before. Obviously, I was being watched. He might be in some obscure place, but he apparently did have someone lurking around outside my house, tracking my every move.

"I was arrested," I confessed, not knowing what else to do. "I promise I won't tell them anything, though. I promise."

"That's right, dead bitch. You won't be alive to tell them anything. Or, maybe I'll let you think about this for a while. Maybe I won't kill you just yet. Maybe I'll just have someone come in during the night and slice up one of your little girls. Maybe I'll put a bomb under your car and watch you explode into flames. It might not even be now. It could be three months or three years from now. You'll always be watching over your shoulder, because I'll strike when you least expect it. Your life is mine now, whore." He cackled as he hung up the phone.

I jumped out of bed and grabbed the girls from their cribs where they were napping and brought them into my bedroom. It didn't have any windows, and I felt like we would be the safest in there. Then, with the strength of a man, I piled as much furniture in front of the sliding glass doors as I could. I kept the curtain open, though, so I could keep watch to make sure that there wasn't anyone back there. I dragged a bureau in front of the entry door, and propped a chair against it, just in case. We were now prisoners in our own apartment. I knew that this guy meant business, and that he must not have any respect for life.

The phone was ringing again, so I answered it. It was Tony, laughing demonically and satisfied, as if he were Satan himself. "That couch is not going to stop my boys from coming in!" He informed me and then hung up the phone. The minute I put the receiver back on the hook it was ringing again. This time it was just laughing. I hung it up and it immediately began to ring. Every time I put it back down it would start again. Endless laughing and endless torture. How was he doing this? Why was he doing this? I thought for sure that ninjas or something were going to burst through the glass at any moment, and that our lives would be over. I prayed for the Lord to help us, and the calls eventually ceased, more than three hours and 300 calls later. When the phone finally stopped ringing and the line became available I called 911 and explained the situation.

The cops showed up 20 minutes later and tried to trace the phone calls. When they were unsuccessful they said that there was nothing else they could do until I knew where this guy was calling from. They promised to do extra surveillance around our apartment, and to keep a presence in the parking lot as much as possible. After all, we were right behind the State Police headquarters. They suggested that we get out of town for a while, but I thought that was too risky. I didn't want to get the rest of my family mixed up in this thing. I feared that Tony's reach may extend up to Massachusetts, and I couldn't bear to see anyone else hurt on my account. I didn't dare tell my mother or father for fear that they would insist that I come home. I needed to resolve this on my own, and not speak a word of it to any of them.

None of us left the house for several days. I didn't sleep, just kept alert, edgy guard the entire time. It wasn't as if I could have stopped an attack, but I felt better eliminating the possibility of being caught by surprise. Finally my nerves calmed down to the point where I could face the possibility of my destruction from venturing out of the confines of the apartment's illusion of safety. I was not going to be held prisoner by this psychopath. As the bright sun hit my now sensitive eyes, I realized how foolish I had been to be gripped by the threats. I voraciously scanned the horizon for unfamiliar people or vehicles, with a heightened sense of awareness that danger could be around any corner. I looked under my car for anything out of the ordinary, and found nothing. I held my breath as I turned the key in the ignition, waiting for a bomb to go off, but none did.

I drove to meet my court appointed attorney, vigilantly conscious of every noise and bump, suspicious of every car that pulled up beside me. I was hopeful that he would have something optimistic to present, but my confidence was dashed at the sight of his downtrodden, besieged demeanor. I was so fucked. I knew that instead of being defended I would only be hindered. This guy was not a fighter, he was a place holder. It was like having a ballerina for a brain surgeon; you just know it's not going to go well.

Chapter 18

By the skin of her teeth

It was the morning of my trial, and still no tape had been presented to my lawyer. The cops kept promising and promising, but there was always some excuse as to why it wasn't available. They had requested that we show up half an hour early to court for the exchange. Everything I needed to prove my innocence was on that recording. I knew that if the judge heard me continuously telling the undercover cop that I was not comfortable, and that I was not going to have sex with him, even offering to return the money, that there would be no possible way for him to find me guilty. It was cut and dry, but apparently only in my childlike, technicolor version of the world where everyone plays by the rules, does what they say they will, and truly wishes to seek justice. Boy, was I in for a rude awakening about how things really happen in America's court system.

Five minutes before court was called into session Detective Miller entered the conference room and announced to us that "unfortunately" the tape had broken that morning, and it would no longer be available as evidence. I was stunned, and felt a sinking in the pit of my stomach. I opened my mouth to protest, but my lawyer covered it and directed me not to anger anyone. He said that we'd be fine without it, but I knew otherwise.

Court was called into session, and I sat near the front listening to the cases that were called before mine. I was very pleased to see that the judge was, in my opinion, quite fair and logical. My spirits rose as I began to believe that this was a man who could recognize that I was an innocent person unwittingly caught in a bad situation who clearly wanted to obey the law. I hoped that he could see that my intentions were pure, and that I was merely a young girl trying to support her family.

The woman whose case was heard directly in front of mine was a three time convicted prostitute and drug addict with a rap sheet a mile long. She had been caught in the act of giving a blow job for $75 in a car at Bryant Park. "Wow," I thought, "that's way worse than what I did." She plead guilty and was given a $75 fine plus court fees. Not only was this judge reasonable, but maybe even a bit lenient.

My heart literally stopped when I saw "Tim Fitz" saunter down the right aisle of the courtroom, smug and beaming with adoration for himself. He was all cleaned up, wearing a suit and tie and a small pair of horn rimmed glasses. He carried a briefcase close to his heart, like he was protecting it with his life. What did it contain, the Holy Grail? Something about seeing him brought me right back to that terrifying moment where I thought my worst fears were going to be realized. I could feel his hand on my jaw, the way my mind raced trying to figure a way

142

out of the situation, and the sinking horror of being completely victimized. I still had not been able to overcome the constant panic attacks I suffered as a result of that night, and this moment was no different. I couldn't breathe. Even though my logic knew that he could no longer hurt me, my emotions kicked into full gear and overrode my sensibility. Seeing him caused a mind numbing visceral reaction that could not have been duplicated if I were being burned at the stake.

It was my turn to go in front of the judge. I stumbled and balked, unable to even get my name out clearly when asked. The mere presence of that man sent incapacitating shockwaves up my spine and rendered me paralyzed. The judge asked me how I was pleading, and I had no idea what to say. He explained my options, and I chose "not guilty" as the one I thought most clearly marked my position. "Tim Fitz" and the County Prosecutor snickered to one another like they'd just been told that the moon was made out of cheese. I tried to tell the judge what had happened, but my attorney quietly scolded me under his breath to shut me up and whispered a warning that my story sounded implausible. I agreed, but insisted that sometimes the truth is stranger than fiction, and that I stood by my words. He asked for a minute off the record with me, which was swiftly denied. The judge reprimanded him, saying that we'd had a month to prepare for the trial and time was up. This was far from correct, but I was helpless and voiceless now. Just when I thought things couldn't get any worse, the prosecution brought forth their "evidence." They confessed that the tape had malfunctioned and was no longer admissible, but pulled out a Polaroid picture as their smoking gun. I stared in disbelief as they displayed a photo of a condom, rolled completely out on the bed, poised and waiting to be applied, as proof that I intended to have sex with my client. I watched the rest of the scene from outside my body, having mentally detached for fear of going insane from the injustice of it all. I wanted to scream aloud. Everyone knows that if you are going to use a condom you unroll it onto the penis, and not before. It would be almost impossible to use that condom now that it had been expanded. If they were going to fabricate something it should at least have been properly thought through. How could the judge miss that point? I didn't stand a snowball's chance in hell. They were all in collusion and had a very clear agenda. This was not a hearing, just a formality. I was found guilty and sentenced to two weeks in jail and a $500 fine plus court costs and attorney fees.

I was stunned, and just stood there in disbelief. What about the blowjob girl? He let her off the hook even with prior convictions. I was clean as a whistle and they were throwing the book at me. It didn't make any sense and I questioned how they could even get away with such a thing in this day and time. It was something that I thought could only happen in the movies. This kind of shit didn't happen to real people…or, did it? In an instant my views on the death penalty changed. I no longer had the luxury of believing in the piousness of the justice system. What if my charges had been more serious? I was just a stupid housewife and mother… what did they have to gain by framing me like this? I wondered what lengths they would have gone through if this had been a high profile case.

The next thing I knew I was waving a quick goodbye to Jack, and they were ushering me behind the court to a holding room where I was to be handcuffed and processed immediately for jail. My lawyer had just shrugged his shoulders and disappeared into the crowd. I was all alone, scared, and confused. By the grace of God, the bailiff noticed that I didn't quite fit the profile and started chatting before he put the cuffs on. He told me that I could appeal the case if I thought it had been incorrect or unfair and that I would be let go until my next court date, during which I would be entitled to opt for a jury trial. He said that my lawyer should have informed me of my rights. He shook his head with disgust, like he'd had this conversation before. "I appeal, then!" I shouted. The kind bailiff opened the door back up and pointed to where I needed to go to file the necessary documents.

Had it not been for this angel sent to protect me, I would have spent the next two weeks in county jail, missing my babies. Instead I was back out in the brisk air, trying to make sense of what had just taken place. I had escaped by the skin of my teeth. I could not help but recognize the irony, though. Instead of the stark reality of grey prison walls, I would be returning home as an emotional prisoner to my marriage.

Chapter 19

Spicing things up

Things between me and Jack were at a breaking point. I felt so betrayed by his indifference towards my safety and wellbeing through the whole escort thing that I had pulled away from him emotionally. I was plagued by the notion that he could allow me to be with other men for monetary gain and not think twice about it. This was not the type of marriage I wanted. He knew that I was becoming bitter and discontent and our sex life had fizzled into oblivion. Even though I was finding it difficult to love him, I wasn't ready for a divorce. I was committed to giving my girls an intact family regardless of what that meant for me. It was a mixture of all of these things that softened the blow when he began suggesting that we pursue a swinging lifestyle. He thought that it would invigorate us to be with another couple, and he began bringing home magazines with personal ads in them. I sort of went along for the ride, but after seriously considering it for a while I began driving the bus. We swapped letters and photos with some people, and eventually

Jack and I started meeting them for drinks to scope out who was available.

The one thing you notice very quickly about swingers is that there is generally an imbalance in the relationship. Typically one person is hot and the other is disgusting. You have to take the good with the bad and try to find a tolerable situation. On our first "dates" I felt like Jack was turning the good looking women off. They all seemed willing to do me, but reluctant to want him there. I knew that if I was going to take the plunge and be with a chick she'd have to be pretty smokin', so I began leaving Jack at home for the initial contacts.

I put on my slinkiest outfit, did my hair and makeup, and drove to meet Ben and Sara at a T G I Friday's late one Saturday evening after the kids had gone to bed. I was pleasantly surprised by how they looked. He was tall, handsome, and far better than what I had at home. She was a petite redhead with a shapely set of implants that caught my attention. For a woman in her late 40's she was quite attractive. We chatted for a while and began to hit it off. It was more of a comfort level than a friendship that I was looking for. We had absolutely nothing in common except for the fact that we were all horny. They'd had a few experiences before, and were looking to add to their resume. By the time we'd finished our second round they were eager to take me home. I called Jack from the pay phone and we were on the way.

They came to our apartment and things were going pretty smoothly except for the fact that I was nervous as shit. This all sounded like a good idea, but I wasn't sure if I could go through with it. I knew I wanted to make out with her, but didn't know if I'd be cool with going down. Ben and Jack sat on the couch talking about racing and Sara began to get aggressive with me. I was sitting on a cushioned kitchen stool. She approached me from behind and started kissing the back of my neck. I was intrigued that she knew exactly what would get me going. She reached around to brush my breasts with her fingertips while her hot breath was beating against the nape of my neck. Her tits were pressed against my back. A huge, warm surge of excitement trickled down the crack of my ass as she came forward to kiss my mouth. I had never kissed a woman before, but it was soft and intriguing. The men were now at full attention as Sara and I gently but passionately made out. It was definitely time for things to move to the next level, so she and I went into the bedroom for a little bit of privacy. I thought it would be more comfortable if we didn't have an audience at first.

Within seconds we were both completely nude and rolling around on the bed. Her skin was like nothing else I had ever felt. It amazed me how supple she was. She started sucking on my nipples and soon two of her fingers were inside my pussy which was throbbing and swollen from all of the anticipation. I was happy to see that she was completely shaved just like me. I wasn't sure how I would react if she'd had a hairy bush. I reached down to stroke her cunt and she moaned with ecstasy. We kissed a bit more, and the next thing I knew, her face was between my legs. I jumped as her tongue touched my clit for the first time. It was completely exciting to look down and see a woman's long, luxurious hair streaming across my legs, and dainty, angelic face buried in my pussy. She lapped it all up like a hungry tiger cub, enthusiastically tonguing my hole and my ass. I can't say that she got me off, but it was still a good time.

I knew that it was my turn now, and it was either sink or swim. I decided to swim. I dove right in and started sucking on her clit. By the way she was letting out little yelps and raising her hips I assumed that I was doing okay for my maiden voyage, but still, I wasn't very confident. I had only tasted my own pussy before, either second hand or off my fingers. I was used to a certain sweetness, but she was tangier than I expected. When I stuck my tongue in her hole and swallowed her sap it almost burned as it went down. It was funny to me that the odor you get on your face and fingers, and what wafts up when a woman begins sweating down there is absolutely nothing like the actual flavor. I was surprised that she was more bitter than fishy. I can't say that I enjoyed it, but Jack sure did when he walked in the room and saw me buried in Sara's womanhood. I knew that I'd pretty much made his life now that he was experiencing girl-girl action for the first time.

The boys were naked in an instant, and soon we were a foursome. Ben started licking me from behind, and Jack stuck his cock in Sara's mouth. Apparently she sucked on it a little too hard because I could detect pain instead of pleasure on his face. We tried all sorts of combinations. It was like a naughty conga line. We had agreed ahead of time that there would not be a full swap, so when it came to actual penetration, we stuck with our spouses. Everyone has their own set of rules, and we thought it best if we didn't quite go all the way, not knowing how it was going to affect us afterwards.

Eventually we were all spent and our new "friends" got dressed and went home. It was interesting, but I was fairly certain that girls were not

150

my thing. Still, it made Jack happy, and that was the main goal, so our evening was a success.

We lay in bed reminiscing about the finer points of that night for the longest time. Reliving it was probably more fun and stimulating than actually doing it, but, at least we now knew. It worried me that even in the midst of every man's fantasy Jack failed to get really hard. Shit, if two women together didn't make that thing stand at attention, what would? It was helpful to see that it wasn't just me, though. Had we not had this experience it would have been easy for me to attribute his limpness to the fact that I wasn't quite the girl I used to be. I was both relieved and concerned. I hated to bring it up, but Jack's growing frustration with this dysfunction was making him weary of even trying to fuck me. Sometimes he would inject his penis with a solution that would allow an erection, but it made his cock as cold as ice, and it wasn't a pleasant experience for me. I didn't like the fact that he had to stick himself with a needle, either. It just seemed like a lot to go through for something that should be natural. It was getting to the point where he didn't want to put himself through the embarrassment of not being able to perform, so he just didn't. I was starting to crave a hard cock, but I was attempting to conceal it in my subconscious as a petty daydream that I had no reason to succumb to.

Jack slipped back into a seething depression and only showed signs of happiness when he was flipping through porn. He became consumed with arranging another rendezvous. Although I'd had fun, once was enough for me. I didn't think I was cut out for eating pussy, and had no interest in trying again.

A few weeks later, my friend Barb was over and we had just about finished a bottle of Merlot when Jack started insisting that we women get it on together. Barb and I were emotionally close, but I wasn't particularly attracted to her. She was in her late 50's and a little rough around the edges, an uneducated country girl, shaken from having gone through a tough marriage to a closet transvestite. She had 5 kids, and was more of a mom type than a sexual being. Still, she jumped right on it, having always wanted to explore her bisexual feelings. The two of them conspired against me and tried to wear me down. If her crotch tasted like Sara's I really didn't think I could go through with it. Besides, I just didn't think of Barb in that way.

The phone began ringing so I went into the bedroom to answer it. When I turned around Barb was right behind me. I sat on the bed and began talking to the person on the other end. It was a friend from high school who I hadn't spoken with in years. Barb seized the opportunity to slide her hand up my thigh and start probing my twat. Her finger felt good as it plunged into my moist darkness. She pulled her finger out and licked it. I could tell by the look in her eyes that she was not going to take no for an answer anymore, and besides, I was horny all of a sudden. I quickly said my goodbyes and promised to call back later, sighting an emergency. Before the phone was even back on the hook, Barb and I were ripping each other's clothes off. Her kiss made me weak. We had an incredible chemistry together. I was intoxicated by her sensuality. We stood naked, looking at our bodies rubbing up against one another in the mirror. It was one of the most passionate experiences of my life. She made me cum over and over again, harder than I'd ever climaxed before. When I went down on her she was sweet and delicious, and I couldn't get enough of her beautiful, writhing body. It was a completely different experience from my first time, and I thoroughly enjoyed it. Still, it really wasn't my thing. I was definitely a straight girl experimenting, and could never see myself wanting a steady diet of women.

My whole world opened up that night, though, and so much became clear. She was amazing and wondrous, even though you never would have guessed it by looking at her. I was inebriated by her touch, and, for the first time in my life, could finally understand why men were such hounds. It was very clear to me that each and every woman, no matter her size, shape, age, or race has something so magical to offer that it might be nearly impossible to turn down the rush of sampling a new one. Her feminine power was overwhelming. I could totally see now why a guy could be helpless against his desires. Having sex with a woman truly can be a supreme high. I don't think that most chicks get that. It blows our minds that men can be such pricks, but when you have been captivated by the magnitude of such an experience it all comes into focus and you have one more piece of the puzzle. Every woman should have at least one bi encounter as part of her education so we can understand what men go through.

The next morning, Jack tried to make love to me, but his cock would have nothing of it. With a very red face he decided to confide in me. "I'm going to have surgery. They're gonna put a pump in my balls that will inflate a rod in my shaft that will allow me to stay hard as long as I want."

"That sounds disturbing; please don't do it," I begged him. "And besides, where are you going to get the money?"

"I've borrowed $10,000 and the operation is already paid for. It's something I've just got to do for myself," he said in a matter of fact manner, as if we had all the money in the world. "I'm going in tomorrow morning."

I could barely believe what I was hearing. We didn't have enough money for diapers and my husband had gone into debt to try to fix his limp dick. How could he be so selfish? I wondered how his priorities had gotten so messed up. Did he really think that this is what it would take to keep me, or was he just worried about how he'd be able to get his next victim if we broke up? This was a pretty big decision, and he hadn't even consulted me. I felt betrayed. I considered packing up the girls while he was in the hospital and taking off. He wouldn't miss us once he had a new cock.

Apparently our discussion had gotten heated enough that the girls heard us and began crying for our attention. As I looked into their big, teary, innocent eyes I knew that running was not an option. I wanted them to have a normal life. I decided to surrender to Jack's authority in order to keep the peace.

Recovery from the operation took three weeks, but the moment that the doctor cleared Jack for takeoff he wanted to try his new contraption out on me. It was like a frankendick, and I was terrified. He had stitches and the whole thing was pitch black from bruising. He wanted me to suck it, but I just couldn't. I was nauseous at the sight of it. I didn't want him to come anywhere near me with it. It was so gross. This was not the reaction that Jack had anticipated, and he got angry and enraged. He forced me to submit my body to him, and I cried as he fucked me with his grotesque, artificial instrument. I was beginning to wonder if maybe I just had no interest in sex at all, with him or any other man. Perhaps my days of being horny and excited were over. I thought it was conceivable that everything I'd been through to this point had turned me away from the feelings I once had, and that I would never desire the company of another man again.

As time passed, I drew further inward. Jack and I were like roommates, and that was fine with me. It was all I could take. He seemed to accept our platonic relationship, as if something were better than nothing. I longed for the days when I had believed there was more to life. I had to do something to dig myself out of this hole before the soil closed in over my head. I needed inspiration. I needed hope. I was no good for the girls like this.

Chapter 20

Windows, siding, and roofs, oh, my…

My second court date came and went. Realizing that I had no choice but to be martyred, I decided to plead "no contest" and move on. We struck a deal which suspended my sentence, and I wouldn't have to serve jail time unless there was another offense. I didn't feel good about it, but I needed the closure.

Eager to take another whack at the job market, I scoured the Sunday edition of the Richmond Times Dispatch classified section. This time it seemed like all of the jobs involved sales, but I was willing to give it a shot. I dialed the number in one of the ads and asked for Mr. Green, as instructed. It turns out that Mr. Green does not exist, but it helps them track which ads they are getting a response from. Tricky little fuckers. The person on the phone told me that the position involved in-home sales of siding, windows, and roofs. I couldn't say that I had any knowledge of those items, other than that they are essential to every home, but I set up an interview for the next afternoon.

The Pacemaster office was a 40 minute drive, but at least it was a legitimate opportunity, so I wasn't about to complain. I met with the general manager, Ken, who was some fast talking hotshot from Omaha, Nebraska where the company is headquartered. He was very excited about the prospects of hiring a woman. Several had tried and failed, but he had a good feeling about me. He explained that the job would entail a lot of travel, including one week a month out of town. He wondered how that would work with young children, but I told him that my husband would be at home full time, so it wasn't an issue for me. The truth of the matter was that I welcomed the escape. Even though the pay was total commission, there was a small draw of $300 a week until I began making sales and didn't need it anymore. This would be particularly helpful during the two weeks of training. Any money was better than nothing, so I accepted the job, even though it was a bit out of my comfort zone.

There were six other people in my training class, all men, and all experienced in sales. I became a quick hit with my sailor's mouth and naughty disposition. The guys loved me, and I got a ton of attention from everyone in the building. It was nice to be popular, and my ego began to soar, almost to the point of where it should have been. One of the greatest lessons I learned from the training was that no one likes an introvert. That really made sense to me. I was quiet and shy, stifled by my circumstances, and not wanting to step on anyone's toes, but a wallflower was not going to make it in this industry. I remembered my days as a dancer, and how much money I had passed by just because I was too scared to ask for it. I wasn't going to make that same mistake again. Inside I was timid, but outside I was going to be dynamic. It was the perfect opportunity to shed the shell I'd been living in and develop all of the latent talents I knew were within me.

Before long it was time for us newbies to go out into the harsh, cruel world and ply our wares. I was teamed up with a guy named Bob. He was kind of cute, married with two small kids, and had a background in engineering sales. He talked too much and was a bit hyper, but I balanced him nicely. They sent us to Emporia, at the southern border of Virginia, to see an old woman in a huge farm house. True to what would become our normal experience, the lady had no clue we were coming. The telemarketers were pretty slick, and generally folks didn't really want us there, but that didn't stop us. It was policy that we spent a minimum of three hours on each appointment, regardless of interest. It seemed daunting, but there was definitely a method to the madness, and it worked.

We were lucky enough to catch Ms. Hudgins out in her yard and engage her in conversation before she put 2 and 2 together and realized who we were. The country people tended to be pretty laid back and friendly, thankful for company of any sort, which made it much easier to gain favor and familiarity with them. The entire first half hour was supposed to be devoted to everything BUT what we were there for. It became a fun game to see how well we could control the dialogue and to figure out different ways to gain the clients' trust. I specialized in small talk, and eventually Bob got to show off his product knowledge. Four hours later, Bob and I had been fed, entertained, and we were driving away with a contract for $35,000 worth of siding to be put on Ms. Hudgins' home. That translated into a $7,000 paycheck for the two of us to split. We had really hit the jackpot.

The next day at the office we were superstars. Dan, our manager, could not be happier, and he made a huge deal of our accomplishment. This, of course, just made us all the more determined to repeat our success. Everyone wanted to partner up with us in hope that the magic would rub off. I ended up making two more sales that first week, and when the check finally came in, it was almost $5,000. That was more money than I'd ever had in my life, and I had earned it. The hours were long, and I generally worked 6 days a week, fifteen hours a day, and clocked about 1500 miles a week. My confidence was soaring, and my personality was naturally becoming more outgoing and assertive as I regained my dignity. No one could talk their way around me, except for Jack.

My mother, thrilled with my success, but sensing trouble in the marriage, suggested that since I was doing so well financially I put aside a little money each week for myself, just in case. I wasn't particularly comfortable with that idea, still under the mind control of my husband, but I knew it was probably good advice. Although Jack and I were getting along better, he was still in his funk. Even though he was only responsible for watching the girls and taking care of the house he wasn't doing a great job at either thing. He was despondent, not showering for days at a time, and the apartment was always a wreck. I would come home at midnight and the girls would still be wide awake, not even having had dinner. I was not allowed to have a checkbook, only a deposit slip on payday. Jack took care of the accounting, and I was not privy to where our money, my earning, was going. Challenging him on those rules was futile, and I became suspicious of his motivation. I found a bank statement about three months into my new job and the balance in the account was less than $200. I was stunned, knowing that our expenses were relatively low and my income was always $1500 or more per week. Something wasn't adding up. My next check was $6,000, so I resolved to put $5,500 in the account and leave $500 out for myself. After all, I never spent any of the money, and I deserved to have some cash on hand.

All hell broke loose when Jack found my pay stub and reconciled it against the deposit. I thought he was going to kill me. He went ripping through my purse looking for the remainder, and took everything I had in there.

"This is going in the bank, you sneaky bitch!" he screamed at me, crazed and delirious, his eyes bulging, his veins popping. He put on his sneakers, grabbed Ashley, and stormed out the door, threatening to never come back. That was his usual pattern when we fought. He would grab my little one and leave, trying to intimidate me that I'd never see Ashley again. This man was insane. I worried about leaving the kids with him at all. I wouldn't put it past him to clean out the apartment and the bank account and just disappear some day. As long as he left the girls, it would be a blessing, but I knew that would never happen. They were his meal ticket.

When Jack returned several hours later I went out into the van and found a six pack of empty bottles. Great…he had been driving around getting drunk with our 1 year old in the car. I didn't dare confront him, he was too volatile. I just tried to play nice and to smooth things out. I threw myself into my work, and cherished the time that I had away from home. Sometimes, in between appointments, I would park my car and watch the normal mothers holding hands with their kids, putting them into grocery carts, or pushing them on the swings at a playground, and I would sob until there were no more tears left to cry. I missed my daughters more than anything, but I knew that our survival depended on my making money, and I was not educationally qualified for a decent paying 9-5 job. I was trapped in a lot of ways.

I began to find solace in my clients. Sometimes during the warm up portion of our appointments I would start opening up about my personal life. It was nice to have people to listen to me, pray with me, and give me advice. My coworkers were great, too. When things were slow or when someone needed help boosting their sales technique we were teamed up into pairs. That meant dozens of hours in the car together. I formed some incredibly close bonds with the guys. I was an inspiration and a mentor to them, but they gave me back just as much as I gave them.

I was tired, overworked, depressed, and hopeless. The financial situation had evened itself out, but, at what cost? I never saw my girls, my husband was hording all of my money, and my life was one endless sales pitch. Jack and I hadn't had sex in months. Sometimes I would try to get him excited, but he had lost his confidence in the bedroom. I wasn't about to beg my own husband to fuck me. He wasn't taking his medicine, either, and I could see a

162

marked difference in his health. I'm sure that had something to do with it. I would argue with him, pointing out that if he really loved me and his daughters he would want to be healthy for us and he would take the damn pills. It was all falling on deaf ears. All he wanted to do was smoke and make sure that I was still under his thumb.

The more and more I confided in strangers, the more they attempted to convince me that I had no future with Jack. Still, I was stubborn, and scared, not knowing what would happen to Alexis and Ashley if we split. I knew I couldn't move back to Massachusetts because the girls needed their dad. Even if he sucked at being a husband he could still play an important role in their lives. I tried to limit the information I was giving my family, just in case we were able to work things out. They still had no idea about the escort service, or even what a lazy bum Jack had become. I had been good at keeping up appearances and making everyone think that things were fine.

Late one afternoon I was sent 80 miles southwest to a small farm town called Danville. I cursed as I made the drive, as it meant that there would be no chance of getting home before 11 PM. The long journey did provide plenty of time to think, though, and I begged God to show me the right path. I didn't necessarily need the easy one, just the correct one. My blood pressure rose as I discovered that my appointment was in a small trailer. There was almost no possibility of a sale because our products were generally more valuable than the entire home, and the banks wouldn't finance them anyway. The front stairs creaked and swayed as I made my way to the door. There wasn't a car in the driveway, so I hoped that they had forgotten and stepped out, or that they were avoiding me. No such luck. Before I could even knock, a heavy set Black woman greeted me. She was pleasant, and eager for conversation. She seemed lonely. It had to have been 100 degrees in that place, and still they were running a space heater. I was "lucky" enough to get the seat right next to it. I was so distracted by the temperature that I almost didn't notice that we weren't alone. There was a hospital style bed in the corner, and a man covered in white sheets. He moved his head to the left and winked, as if to say hello. I went over to shake his hand, but it was limp and lifeless, just laying there with no feeling. It was as if this poor man's body had given up but his soul still inhabited it, a hostage of his circumstance. I tried to react as if I ran into this sort of situation all the time, not wanting to make a fuss or embarrass these fine people. The woman and I sat down again and started chatting. Apparently the guy had been quite a lady's man in his day. At one time she'd been lucky to snag him. He had a super job with Phillip Morris, but now they were living off of his disability payments. Over the past year, life had become one long hospital visit for the two of them. He had been through dozens of surgeries, and the doctors were always amputating something. That's when I realized that the bed was empty where the man's legs should have been. Shit... I couldn't imagine what a day must have been like for these two, and it didn't look like it was going to get better any time soon. In situations like this I tried to be positive and uplifting, and attempted to add a breath of fresh air for people who were shut in and cut off from the rest of the world. I could tell that my visit was the most exciting thing that had happened to them in a long time. They seemed pretty normal, and I couldn't help wondering how they had gotten to this place. As if reading my mind, the woman answered my question before I had the guts to ask it. "Diabetes," she said. "His sugar got him."

As far as I was concerned, God had brought me here to show me what my future might look like. If Jack didn't take care of himself I would end up the nursemaid to an amputee. I was only 22, and that didn't quite seem like the "happily ever after" I had once envisioned. The worst part was that it was all preventable. If he would just put down those fucking cigarettes and take his damn pills he would probably be okay, but he refused. I would do anything to help him and stand by him, but he needed to put forth the simplest of efforts to ensure that he was at least as healthy as possible going forward. I was hurt and angry that Jack didn't care enough about me and the girls to try to spare us all from the prospect of losing him slowly and painfully in this way. I hugged them both and started the long journey home. I affirmed my resolve to encourage Jack to live a healthier lifestyle and to take the necessary precautions to soften the blow of his disease.

My thoughts of care and concern rushed to a screeching halt when I returned home to find Jack sitting in the chair, cigarette burning in his mouth, ash to his lip, sound asleep and snoring. The babies were on the floor crawling around, completely unattended. The only sign of them having been fed was an empty can of green beans on the table. It was almost midnight and he hadn't bothered putting the kids to bed. I was disgusted. He really had become worthless, even as a parent. I put the girls in their cribs, pulled the Marlboro from his lips, and went to sleep. He was still there at 5AM when I got up for work, completely oblivious to the fact that he ever had any responsibility. I kicked the leg of the chair and he awoke with a start when I left for the office at 7.

"That's a fine how do you do so early in the morning," he scolded me.

"Some of us have obligations," I snapped back, and slammed the door behind me.

That must have pissed him off because I had only been at the office for 10 minutes when the secretary ran in frantically, warning me that Jack was ranting and raving and telling Ken all sorts of crazy stuff, trying to get me fired. All I could hear were things like "whore" and "convict," but I didn't care because Jack had left the girls sitting in their car seats with the keys in the ignition of the minivan. I jumped in and drove away with them, trying to formulate a plan. Barb lived right around the corner, so I dropped the girls off with her for safekeeping, and went back to work. By then Ken had threatened to call the police if Jack didn't leave and he was sitting on the curb smoking.

"We'll talk about this later," I told him, tossing him the keys to his vehicle. "Go the fuck home and stop trying to mess with my life!"

I knocked on the office door and the secretary unlocked it so I could enter. The whole place was silent, awestruck by the display. "I told you he's an asshole," I said, shrugging my shoulders, and we began our morning meeting. I couldn't let an outburst like this ruin my day. I had money to make, and a family to support.

The appointments were close today, which was a blessing. I was assigned to a single woman in a small cedar ranch who needed replacement windows. She could tell something was wrong the moment I got there. When she asked me what was troubling me I just burst into tears. I told her the whole story, from start to finish, as inappropriate as that was. Without hesitation she told me that I needed to leave Jack and never look back. She called Jack a piece of shit and warned me that he would only get worse and that my situation was just going to deteriorate. I knew she was right, but leaving him was easier said than done.

I composed myself long enough to show her the windows, and then went and measured her order. When I pulled out my calculator to total everything up, a small piece of paper fell out. It was the message from a fortune cookie. It read: "Many people receive advice; only the wise ones follow it." How poignant…

Chapter 21

La, la, la, la…I can't hear you

I rushed home to confront Jack, finally secure in what I needed to do. He was sitting on the couch smoking a cigarette as if nothing had happened. He never even asked where the girls were.

"Are you serious?" I screamed at him. "You pull shit like that and try to get me fired and you don't even have anything to say???"

"There's nothing to say. I'm sick of you running around all hours of the night, having fun, doing whatever you want while I take care of the kids." I could tell that Jack actually believed what he was saying and felt totally justified in his thinking.

I couldn't understand how he could even accuse me of such a thing. I'd been busting my ass to support him, and he obviously didn't appreciate it. He acted as if he had been doing me a favor. "We're over," I told him. "I can't do this anymore. You don't work, you don't take care of the house, you're neglecting the girls, and, to top it all off, you won't even fuck me. I'm done." I was proud of myself for finally standing up and admitting that the situation was no longer acceptable.

"Well, that's tough shit. You're stuck with me. The only way out of this is to kill me because I'll never give you a divorce," he gloated, picking up a knife and taunting me to stab him. I truly wished I could. "If you want to go fuck other guys then do it, but you will always be my wife."

"You are not my husband anymore, and even if you won't sign the papers I am divorcing you from my heart right now. And, if I feel like fucking someone I will be sure to do it because, from this day forward, I am a single woman."

I grabbed some clothes and some supplies for the girls and took off. I stopped at a payphone to call the office and let them know where I was, and then called Barb. She was available to baby sit, and offered to have us stay with her for a few days. It was just what I needed, and I took her up on it.

Things were quiet until Jack showed up in the parking lot at work again. He was finally remorseful and promised that he had had a change of heart. He wanted to try to work things out, but needed for me and the girls to come home. Like an optimistic asshole, I agreed. We decided to get some counseling, and Jack quit smoking. He even started taking his medication. Maybe he really had changed? I was very open with him and explained that I was in desperate need of some sex. He told me that he was emotionally unable, and that he was okay with my getting it elsewhere. I didn't know exactly how that could be, but I wasn't going to argue. I needed to find out if I even had sexual feelings anymore. They had been squashed for so long that I didn't know whether or not I was permanently damaged.

A few nights later I worked until about 10 PM. When I made my last call in to the office, my manager, Dan, told me that there was a little party going on and invited me to join them for a drink or two on my way home. It was just what I needed. Jack had been putting the girls to bed at nine since our argument, so I knew that there was no rush in my getting back.

The telemarketing crew had broken out a few cases of beer while waiting for the last sales people to check in for the night, and things were getting pretty crazy. Dan gave me a Miller Light and we toasted to my high sales. It went down very easily, and soon we were toasting much sillier things alone in Dan's office. To be honest, Dan was not one of my favorite people. He was kind of a pompous jerk. All the chicks dug him because he was tall, athletic, and handsome, but he was also very married. That didn't stop him, though. It was no secret that he had a steady girlfriend in Roanoke who he would see frequently. Still, tonight, he was just what the doctor ordered. I quickly weighed the pros and cons of letting the night progress. I liked the fact that we were both married because it meant that neither of us could get very attached, and that whatever happened would be purely physical. I also felt better knowing that he was already cheating. That way I didn't have to feel guilty about being a home wrecker.

Before I knew it, Dan was sticking his tongue down my throat. Oh, my God, it was incredible. Everything I feared had died inside me was now bubbling up to the surface. It felt so good to kiss someone that deeply, and with such enthusiasm. We were like two little kids on Christmas, tearing open packages. Dan swept his arm across his desk, knocking everything on it to the floor. He lifted me up and laid me on it, spreading my legs and pushing aside my panties with his nose. He poured beer on my pussy and feverishly lapped it all up. When he couldn't help but know that I'd cum, he plunged all 10 inches of his thick cock deep inside me while holding my ankles on either side of his head. I experienced several minutes of pure bliss. I could barely remember why I thought I could go without sex for even a day. He fucked me with all of his might, and I loved it. When he was done he pulled out and spewed all over my tits. I rubbed it into my sweaty skin and then he licked it off. His cock was still hard, so I sat him in his leather chair and sucked him until he blew again. He was insatiable, and so was I. Suck, fuck, repeat. That was our pattern until both of us were so spent that we could no longer move. We collapsed together on the prickly rug and held one another while we regained our senses. The office reeked of beer, pussy, and seamen. Things were strewn everywhere. We hobbled out, not giving a shit about much else other than getting a few hours of sleep before work tomorrow and making sure we were put together enough to face our spouses.

I listened to the same song over and over again the entire ride home, singing along with the lyrics as loudly as I could. "Well, I'm shameless... when it comes to loving you...I'll do anything you want me to, I'll do anything at all ...and I'm standing here for all the world to see, oh baby, that's what's left of me...don't have very far to fall..." I was happy. I was satisfied. I was finally alive again. There was no way in hell I could stay with Jack. I knew I didn't want Dan, but I did want to feel young and vibrant again, and I knew that it wasn't going to happen with Jack.

Everyone was asleep when I crept in. I took a shower and plopped down on the couch to sleep for an hour before I got dressed. It was almost time to go back to work. I didn't have much of an opportunity to rest, but I knew the adrenaline rush would carry me through the day. I had been reborn.

Jack woke up and sat with me as I was getting ready. "What I said about you fucking other guys...I've thought about it, and I wasn't being honest. It would kill me if you did that."

Oh, shit!!! That was certainly not what I wanted to hear. It had always been agreed that I would have that freedom, and now he was changing the rules. "I have to tell you that I can't be monogamous with you anymore," I advised him in a low, terrified tone, afraid of how he would react. "I need something in my life to look forward to, or I'm gonna go crazy."

"We can try," he pleaded. "I'll make sure you get what you need."

We went back and forth. I tried to be as tactful as I possibly could while still getting my point across. The marriage just wasn't working for me anymore. Jack refused to accept that, and vowed once again that he would never set me free. It was as if I was his possession.

"Fine, then," he relinquished. "Go be a whore, but you will never get away from me. This is forever, whether you like it or not."

I was crying out of frustration at this point. I told him that I didn't wish to be married any longer, and that we needed to make arrangements to separate. In my heart I knew that he wasn't going to give up easily. He had no future without me. I was his sole support. He didn't want to work, and he certainly didn't have the energy to replace me. Jack started screaming something about how much alimony I was going to have to pay him, and how I was going to lose the girls. With that I walked out the door and headed to the office, happy to be rid of him, at least for most of the day.

Over the next several months I behaved as if I were single. I fucked who I wanted to fuck, and made no excuses. I figured that if I flaunted this in Jack's face he would see that there was no sense in trying to reconcile. I hoped that if it got bad enough or painful enough for him that he would just give up and grant me a divorce. Instead he gained strength from my actions because he could truly identify himself as a victim of my abuse. Obviously, my method was not the most mature, but I was at a loss for any other ideas. Little by little I began breaking the news to my family. They seemed distant and cold, and it didn't make sense until I eventually realized that Jack was in close contact with them, slyly spoon feeding them the details of my folly, making me look like I was being a bad mother and an unfaithful wife, not giving them the whole story. He pretended that he had been a solid support for me, and that no matter what he did it wasn't enough. They began having sympathy for him and distain for me. He told them that I was out every night until the wee hours, but never mentioned that it was because of my work schedule, and it was how I was sustaining our financial responsibilities. He secretly tapped the phone and played them conversations between me and other men, telling my family that I was a slut, more interested in sex than motherhood, but never mentioning that we had agreed that I could do so, and never revealing that he had no issue with it as long as I came back with money, like when he was pimping me out. My family was horrified at who they thought I'd become.

Jack and I fought on a daily basis. He was angry that I was not relenting in my request for a divorce, that he no longer had power over me. Late one night when I returned from work he began taunting me. He revealed that he would be leaving and taking the girls with him. Apparently, my mother, thinking that she had aligned herself with the moral part of the equation, had offered to buy Jack a house in Massachusetts for him and the girls so he could escape my vile wrath and get his life back in order. She was going to get him a lawyer, and fight to make sure that he was awarded full custody. I was furious as I began to uncover all of the ways he had deceived them. I was hurt that they had fallen for his charade, but knew that I had helped perpetuate the lie by protecting him all these years. It was time for me to reveal my truth. I had no choice. I was about to lose everything.

For the first time in years, I tried to be as open and honest with my mother as I possibly could. I started from the beginning and told her how my relationship with Jack had begun. We discussed the downfall of Jack's business, and how I'd tried to make him aware of what he was doing that could possibly create what eventually happened. We spoke about how he had been unwilling and unable to keep a job. I revealed the whole escort service thing, not leaving out my responsibility for getting into it, but telling her how I wanted to quit as soon as I knew what the real story was. I told her about getting arrested, being threatened with death by my boss, and being convicted in court. I told her about the swinging we had done, and about Jack's promise from the very onset of our marriage that I would be held harmless for any infidelity if I chose that path. I didn't sugar coat anything, or try to make myself look like a hero, I just explained the facts. I needed her to see how Jack had skillfully manipulated her, just as he had manipulated me.

She was shocked that I had kept all of these things from her, and wondered how I had gotten through them on my own. It hadn't been easy, and, embarrassing as it was, I was relieved that everything was now out in the open. If she was willing to lend a hand then maybe she could help us both. It was never my intention to hurt Jack, just to make him understand that we couldn't go on like this. I wanted to see him happy, healthy and back on his feet again, and I knew that I was perpetuating his misery by allowing him to feed off of me. It was important that he get back out into the world and make his own living. He needed to regain his self-respect, just as I had. I still loved him, but was no longer "in love." I had been wounded beyond repair in the marriage, but I still appreciated the fact that he had given me two beautiful children, and had taught me plenty of life lessons that would enable me to more accurately identify what it was that I did want from a relationship. I knew that the grass would not be greener somewhere else, but it would be *my* grass.

Chapter 22

Mom to the rescue

Doors had been closing for my mother in Boston, and we decided that the best thing that she could do to help me and Jack put the pieces of our marriage back together would be for her to move to Richmond. She offered to rent a house big enough for all of us to live in so that we wouldn't have the hefty financial responsibility of our expensive apartment. We could all live together and split the cost, with her bearing the majority of it. She would help with daycare for the kids, and Jack and I would both be able to work full time. It sounded like the perfect plan. I was hopeful that once Jack started feeling better about himself as a man he would begin to act like the guy I'd fallen for. I was willing to try to put our marriage back together if he would make an effort. I rededicated myself to him and him alone, giving up my scandalous affairs, and opening up to our union as a couple.

It was a huge adjustment for all of us. My mother had gotten used to her privacy, and wanted everything to be kept a certain way. She laid down the ground rules, and introduced structure back into our lives. I will always be grateful for the sacrifice she made for us, uprooting herself and changing her entire world so that we would have a chance to rebuild our lives as a family. The girls loved having her around, and it was wonderful to have the companionship.

One of the concessions I agreed to make in order to salvage the marriage was to leave Pacemaster, and everyone I'd been screwing there. I made a fresh start with a new company in the same field. The money wouldn't be quite the same, but the hours were more reasonable, and I would have a chance to spend more time with the girls.

Jack got a job at a convenience store, and he seemed to cheer up for a while. Although he was undoubtedly thankful for my mother's contribution having saved our marriage, he was now jealous of the time that she and I were spending together. He was paranoid that it was all a trap to push him out of the picture. If my mom and I were sitting, having a cup of tea, he would hide behind the door in order to eavesdrop on our conversations. I tried to reassure him that the thing I wanted most was for us to be a solid family again. I wanted my kids to grow up with both parents, and to be secure. We just needed to take advantage of this opportunity to put some money aside so that we could eventually get our own place again without feeling the desperate strain we'd been under before. I tried to initiate sex with him whenever possible so he would know that I was committed to him, and also so that we could reestablish the physical bond we once had.

Even though Jack now had a paycheck coming in, he refused to shell out for his portion of the bills. I couldn't figure out what he was doing with his money, but he certainly wasn't supporting the household in any way. It seemed like every little thing set him off. If my mother asked him to mow the lawn he looked at her like her mind had gone bad. When it came time to rake leaves he was nowhere to be found. I couldn't believe that he was not enough of a man to hold up his tiny scrap of the responsibility. I think he always viewed my mother as a woman of means, and felt like she owed us her support because she had so much. This was hardly the case, though. Whatever my mother had came because she worked extremely hard, long hours, and managed her money well; forgoing the things she wanted to do for herself.

Jack became a constant source of upheaval in the house. He would come home from work, slam things around, and scream at all of us. When I disagreed with him, he would pack his bags and threaten to abandon me and the girls. They would be crying and tugging at the cuffs of his pants. I think he got a sick charge out of their anguish. I secretly prayed that he would follow through with his plans and that this nightmare would end. At first my mom just went up into her bedroom and shut the door, not wanting to subject herself to his temper. When Jack's outburst started occurring more frequently she began to stand up to him.

"I grew up in an abusive household with an angry father, and you are not going to put me back in another one!" my mother warned him "This house is in my name, and if you can't be a positive influence here, then you're going to have to leave. You can't constantly be pulling this shit on us."

With that, Jack grabbed Ashley and disappeared for three days. He called me in between to let me know that she was safe, but I still worried for her, not knowing what his mental stability was. Of course, he didn't show up for work, either, so he was fired from his job. It didn't make much of a difference, though, because he wasn't contributing to our welfare.

Inevitably, after each time one of these episodes happened, he would come back with some sob story and empty promises to get better and be more valuable in the household. We were all frustrated and emotionally worn down. The girls never knew when there would be an outburst, or when Ashley would be kidnapped and held for "ransom." Poor Alexis always wondered why her father never chose her. In her juvenile mind she imagined that he must love her less. Jack was sick in the head, and it was affecting us all. The girls both loved their dad, in spite of what he was inflicting upon us, and I was caught in the middle. Luckily, my head was clear enough to now realize that my best chance for survival was to stick with my mother. She was really the one who made me see that the way he was treating us all was unacceptable.

It all came to a head one snowy December evening, right before Christmas. Jack had packed his bags out of the blue, and was bitching about something. My mother came down the stairs to confront him. I scurried off with the girls and made sure they were safe in their room before rejoining the discussion. Jack wanted to talk to me alone, but my mother insisted upon staying. I was glad because he always twisted everything and made me feel bad for him, and I was unable to stand strong. His control over me was debilitating, and I needed my mother to help me wade through all of Jack's bullshit. I knew that she always had my best interest in mind, and that of the girls. There was no benefit to her breaking up my marriage; it would only make her burden greater. Jack started on another one of his violent, delusional rants. Once again, my mother cautioned him that she would ask him to leave if he couldn't speak in a rational manner, and once again he flew off the handle. This time he punched his fist through a closet door. With the strength of 10 men, my mother grabbed him by his coat, pushed him out the door, threw his bags on the porch, and locked the deadbolt behind him, slapping her hands together as if to say "job over." He would not be allowed back into the home, even to collect the rest of his belongings, and thus we began our formal separation. It was tough, but it felt like a huge burden had been lifted. I knew it was a positive step, and that it was a new beginning for me. My journey as Jack's wife had run its course, and now it was time to start healing.

Chapter 23

How did I get here?

I was not so naïve as to believe that Jack would let me go just like that. Our divorce took more than three tumultuous years. Every chance he got, Jack stirred the pot. He moved to a fleabag motel about 40 miles away, out in Bum Fuck Egypt, and that's where the girls had to spend every other weekend. Luckily, they were too young to know that it was a bad situation, and they went along like champs. I was terrified the whole time they were gone because his "neighbors" were less than upstanding citizens.

Jack went about punishing me by trying to make the girls hate me. He told them graphic details of our situation even though they were toddlers. He would also weep in front of them and say that he was going to die because he was so lonesome not having them all the time and that it would be their entire fault if he were to kill himself. Ashley, in particular, was inconsolable when he would bring her home. She would stand at the door for hours, crying huge, mournful tears. When I attempted to comfort her, she would have nothing of it, just sob harder. We literally had to pry her tiny little fingernails out of the woodwork around the front door to get her to move to another room. She wouldn't eat or sleep. She was a wreck, and it really wore on my heart. I loved her so much, but she didn't seem to want any part of me. I began feeling like I was hurting her by not allowing her to live with her dad. Alexis was stoic, not wanting to see either of us upset. She concealed her feelings, but I knew she was in pain.

I had started out with the greatest of intentions, but now my whole world was upside down. In spite of how much anguish I felt over the failure of my marriage, I knew that I still had a chance to succeed. After all, it was as if I'd been given a new lease on life, and I had to make something of myself so that it would all be worth while. I studied for and received my real estate license, and embarked upon a completely new career. I was hired by the most respected agency in town, and Jack made sure that they knew all of the graphic details about my past. Much to my surprise, they didn't care. In fact they nurtured me a bit more, knowing what I'd been through.

I started going out and socializing, and had real friends for the first time in my history. The weight I had gained with the pregnancies seemed to melt away, and I looked amazing. I vowed never to let another man hold me down again. I was going to make my own decisions and carve my own path. Following that path included making peace with Jack, in spite of my mother's wishes. No matter how he tried to slander or usurp me, I attempted to be the bigger person, if only for the benefit of my daughters.

Ashley's mental state continually deteriorated, so once Jack got on his feet and moved into suitable housing, I agreed to let her go live with him. He had gotten what he wanted. He had managed to obtain half of the children. He couldn't leave without getting his share, even though little lives were at stake. He started dating trashy women with solid jobs. They were assholes, just like me. Even though he had little to offer, the women seemed more than pleased to take care of him. Go figure....

I was not happy about seeing the girls split, but, in a sense, it was the best of both worlds. Each girl grew up as an "only child," with the complete focus of one parent, yet they both had a sister on the weekends. It was fucked up, but it worked for us.

I relished my new found freedom and power. I felt young. I felt beautiful. I felt invincible. The shy, portly girl from Holden, Massachusetts was gone, for better or worse. This was not a course that I would have imagined in a million years, but, for a change, it felt promising. For all that I suffered, and for all that I had been through, I had made it to the light at the end of the tunnel. I had life by the balls, or perhaps it had me. In any event, I was able to hold my head high, breathe deeply, and face the challenge of the new day. This time I was going to try my best not to fuck up, no matter how appealing that prospect was. But, we forget so quickly. My second attempt at marriage, and the years which follow require their own book.

www.ingramcontent.com/pod-product-compliance
Lightning Source LLC
Chambersburg PA
CBHW021230090426
42740CB00006B/470